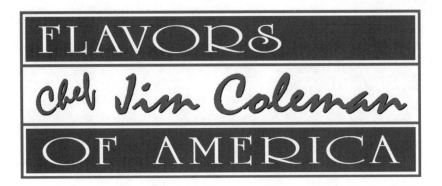

FLAVORS
chef Jim Coleman
OF AMERICA

by
Jim Coleman and **Candace Hagan**
with Greg Slonaker

In Association with the Rittenhouse Hotel

Photographs by Tom Frkovich
Illustrations by Adriano Renzi

Camino Books, Inc.
Philadelphia

Manufactured in the United States of America

1 2 3 4   01 00 99

Coleman, Jim.
        Flavors of America   /   Jim Coleman and Candace Hagan, with Greg Slonaker.
                    p.   cm.
        Includes index.
        ISBN 0-940159-52-X (pa. : alk. paper)
        1. Cookery, American.   2. Cookery, International.   I. Hagan,
    Candace.   II. Slonaker, Greg.   III. Title.
    TX715.C692   1999
    641.5973—dc21   99–12319

Many of the designations used by manufacturers and sellers to distinguish their products are
claimed as trademarks. Where those designations appear in this book and Camino Books, Inc.,
was aware of a trademark claim, the designations have been printed in caps or initial caps.

Author photograph © Tom Frkovich
Cover and interior design: Jerilyn Bockorick

Pictured on cover (*clockwise from top left*): Herbed Roasted Chicken Breast with Citrus Butter and
Mushroom Ragout; Minestrone; Clams in Apple Cider; A Traditional Chesapeake Crab Bake

This book is available at a special discount on bulk purchases for promotional, business, and
educational use.

For information write:

Camino Books, Inc.
P.O. Box 59026
Philadelphia, PA 19102
http://www.caminobooks.com

CONTENTS

FOREWORD

The *Flavors of America* television series was created to enlighten viewers in an entertaining way about the diversity of American cooking. These programs provide an in-depth look into the origins of regional cuisine and the ethnic culinary traditions that enrich our country. Viewers are encouraged to try the exceptional recipes prepared by chef Jim Coleman, whose engaging personality and technical skills entice home cooks to join him in the kitchen. On some of the shows, Jim plays host to renowned regional chefs who display their specialties.

This companion cookbook is a permanent collection of *Flavors of America* recipes that provides you with more detailed historical information on the topics featured in the television series. The stunning photographs, taken right on the set, are reminders of how the finished dishes should look.

Jim Coleman's philosophy is that cooking should be fun. We encourage you to watch the program, use the book, and enjoy the experience of gourmet home cooking using the many bounties of this wonderful country.

Jim Davey
Executive Producer
Flavors of America

ACKNOWLEDGMENTS

This book would not have been possible without the help of a number of special people. The authors are grateful to the following individuals for their contributions:

David Benton, vice president and general manager of the Rittenhouse Hotel, for believing in and supporting this and all projects;

Jim Davey, the kind of partner everyone wishes for;

Stanley Keenan, the true pastry chef behind the recipes— just too covered in chocolate to put on television;

Melissa Jacobs, because every project needs a queen;

Raul Schmalzbach, our future Spielberg and writer;

Lori Simon, for last-minute help on things we needed yesterday;

Lou Miraglia, who continued to be a big help through his many vacation days;

Keith Wagner, for knowing how to draw the line;

The staff of the Rittenhouse, sorry the schedules are late;

David Othmer and David Rubinsohn, the two Davids who are true visionaries;

James and Margaret Coleman, for being the most supportive parents in the world;

Michelle, Katie, and Jimmy, for their love, support, and understanding throughout this project.

INTRODUCTION

As executive chef at the Rittenhouse Hotel in Philadelphia, one of my goals is to present each guest with food they will remember for a long time. My staff and I spend long hours creating elegant and intricate dishes designed to make every meal a special occasion. This brings me a lot of joy, and I want others to discover the same kind of satisfaction and fun in the kitchen.

The way I cook at the hotel, however, is not the way most people cook at home. So when I sat down to plan the recipes for *Flavors of America*, I made a list of the things that matter most to me when I want to share my enthusiasm about cooking with others. First of all, I like food that is interesting to prepare, which is why we included so much about food history in the book. In addition, I wanted recipes that would inspire but not overwhelm home cooks, and I tried to use ingredients that people can find easily. My most important consideration was that I wanted to offer recipes that make cooking an enjoyable experience.

My focus on the television show *Flavors of America* (and in this book, which is based on that show) is to emphasize that the ability to cook great food is not limited to a few knowledgeable professionals. I try to entice people into the kitchen by demonstrating that cooking does not have to be intimidating, and that the whole process is really a lot of fun.

So come join me in the kitchen and share the many rewards that come from experimenting with techniques and ingredients from the world over, which have come together here to create the *Flavors of America*. This book focuses on the fabulous foods of the Mid-Atlantic, an area that in many ways mirrors the cultural melting pot that is this country. My hope is that after viewing the show and using the book, you will feel like you have savored the culinary riches of this historic and productive region. Enjoy your delicious journey!

Jim Coleman

BEEF, AN AMERICAN CLASSIC

Beef is featured on the menus of most nations, but nowhere is it more appreciated than in the United States. The average American consumes twice as much as his European counterpart and 90 percent more than the typical Japanese diner. Consequently, the U.S. has grown to be the world's largest beef producer, not only satisfying America's craving but also supplying much of the rest of the world.

The mammoth American beef industry that stampeded into the world market was made possible by the favorable agricultural conditions here and the millions of acres of prairie stretching across the country. Such excellent cattle-grazing land was an untapped resource before Columbus arrived, when the closest thing to a beef meal was the barbecued buffalo enjoyed by Native Americans. Cattle made their home on the range only after being shipped in by beef-loving Europeans.

As herds began to flourish, the cow staked its culinary claim by becoming the symbol of one of the more romantic chapters in American history. Cowboys and cattle drives pioneered the mystique of the American West. They branded our culture with frontier spirit and offered anyone who cut into a steak an association with the wide-open spaces. By 1854, the year the first Texas Longhorns made the long trip to New York City, *Harper's Weekly* reported that steak was America's favorite meal.

Over 10 million longhorns were driven from Texas to stockyards in the North in the years between the Civil War and the turn of the century. The hardy breed was chosen for its durability on the trail, but in time its popularity almost caused its extinction. When refrigerated railroad cars simplified beef transit and Western cattlelands became laced with barbed wire fences, the cattle drive became a thing of the past. Ranchers no longer needed cattle with the stamina of the longhorn and began to experiment with other breeds. The King Ranch in Texas is famous for developing exceptional herds by crossing several types of cattle, such as Angus, Santa Gertrudis, and Brahman.

As significant as beef is to our diet, it has been the subject of some controversy. For health's sake, Americans have been cautioned to cut back on saturated fat, and as a result, consumption of beef has gone down. But because beef is such a good source of protein, B-complex vitamins, iron, and zinc, many nutritionists are reluctant to ban it from diets and instead recommend smaller portions and meals with more variety than those once served from the chuck wagon.

Chefs around the country are experimenting with new ways to incorporate moderate amounts of beef in mouthwatering presentations. Consumers can even satisfy their craving for beef by sampling various world cuisines that use this meat as a flavoring agent instead of as the main ingredient. With an eye on moderation and diversity, there's no need to be fenced in when it comes to enjoying this longtime American classic.

MORSEL

Healthy Hamburgers

The sometimes deadly E. coli *bacteria made headlines when it found its way into the American beef supply, specifically in hamburger meat. Further unfortunate incidents can be avoided simply by cooking ground beef thoroughly before it is eaten.*

This bacteria is often found on the outside surface of beef cuts. Steaks and roasts, which are browned on the outside, are free of the bacteria regardless of how rare they are inside. But hamburgers are another story. The outside surface of the beef is mixed throughout when the meat is ground, and it must be uniformly cooked to eliminate the bacteria. E. coli is killed when it reaches a temperature of 160°F, so a hamburger cooked medium-well to well-done (no pink in the middle) is safe to eat.

Researchers are experimenting with the feeding schedules of cattle as well as with meat processing in an effort to significantly reduce the possibility of E. coli *contamination. In the meantime, play it safe, give your meat plenty of time on the grill, and enjoy your hamburgers.*

MORSEL

Mouthwatering Marinades

Marinades, which can do wonders to enhance the flavor of foods, come in as many variations as there are chefs who make them. They vary from thin washes to thick pastes and are flavored with a myriad of sweet or sour, spicy or herbal ingredients. When food is steeped in these pungent mixtures, it acquires a little more personality without losing its own inherent characteristics.

Many marinades contain an acid-based ingredient, such as fruit juice, vinegar, or wine, that not only imparts a distinctive flavor but also acts as a tenderizer. Marinating food should be placed in a non-reactive container such as glass, ceramic, or stainless steel and should be stored in the refrigerator while the marinade is at work.

Marinades were as popular thousands of years ago as they are today. The earliest versions consisted of nothing more than salted water, which worked as a food preservative. In fact, seawater may have been the first marinade, because the word itself comes from the Latin marina, *or "of the sea."*

MARINATED STEAK SALAD WITH A ROASTED RED PEPPER VINAIGRETTE

4 servings

Ingredients for the Beef Marinade

1 1/2 pounds top round steak

1/4 cup olive oil

1/4 cup soy sauce

1/4 cup rice wine vinegar

1 tablespoon chopped fresh garlic

2 green onions, chopped

1 tablespoon finely chopped fresh ginger

1 tablespoon finely chopped lemon grass

Ingredients for the Salad

1 whole red bell pepper

1/2 cup rice wine vinegar

1 clove garlic, peeled and finely chopped

1 teaspoon chopped shallots

salt and pepper to taste

1 1/2 cups olive oil

1/4 pound baby spinach, washed

1/4 pound watercress, washed

Method

- Place the steak in a flat, non-reactive container. Combine the rest of the marinade ingredients in a bowl, then pour over the steak, turning the meat once or twice. Cover and marinate overnight.

- Discard the marinade. Grill or broil the steak on both sides until cooked to taste. After cooking, allow the beef to rest for 10 to 15 minutes. Cut the meat in thin slices across the grain.

- Place the bell pepper under the broiler or over an open flame and blacken the outside, turning occasionally. When the entire pepper is charred, remove it from the heat and place in a plastic bag. Tightly close the top of the bag and allow the pepper to steam in its own heat for about 20 minutes. After removing it from the bag, peel the black skin off the pepper.

- Place the peeled roasted pepper, vinegar, garlic, shallots, salt, and pepper in a food processor and pulse until combined. Slowly add the olive oil, and process until thoroughly mixed together.

- Toss the greens with the dressing and divide among 4 salad plates. Arrange the beef slices around the greens and serve.

GRILLED TENDERLOIN

4 servings

Ingredients

4 8-ounce tenderloin filets

1/4 cup olive oil

2 1/2 cups red wine

1/2 red onion, chopped

1/2 carrot, peeled and chopped

2 celery stalks, chopped

2 teaspoons salt

3 black peppercorns, cracked

2 cloves garlic, crushed

3 whole cloves

1 teaspoon chopped fresh thyme

1 teaspoon chopped fresh rosemary

1 bay leaf

5 juniper berries, crushed

Method

• Place the beef in a flat, non-reactive container. Combine the rest of the ingredients and pour over the beef, turning the meat once or twice. Marinate overnight in the refrigerator.

• Preheat the grill. Preheat the oven to 350°F.

• Grill the tenderloins for approximately 1 to 2 minutes on each side. Finish the meat in the oven until cooked to taste.

BEEF STEW

6 servings

Ingredients

2 tablespoons olive oil

2 pounds cubed beef chuck or top round steak

2 large onions, chopped into 1 1/2-inch chunks

4 cloves garlic, chopped

1 8-ounce can tomato paste

1/4 cup all-purpose flour

1 cup dry red wine

5 1/2 cups beef broth

1 teaspoon Worcestershire sauce

2 large potatoes, peeled and cut into 1-inch cubes

2 bay leaves

1/2 teaspoon dried thyme

1/2 teaspoon ground cumin

2 tomatoes, seeded and diced

6 celery stalks, cut into 1-inch cubes

2 carrots, peeled and cut into 1-inch cubes

1 10-ounce package frozen peas

1 tablespoon chopped fresh rosemary

1 tablespoon chopped fresh parsley

salt and pepper to taste

Method

• Heat the olive oil in a 6-quart stockpot. Add the meat and brown on all sides for approximately 5 minutes.

• Add the onions and garlic and cook for another 2 minutes. Add the tomato paste and cook for an additional 2 minutes. Stir in the flour and cook, stirring, for 1 minute. Deglaze the pot by pouring in the wine and broth and scraping up any browned bits on the bottom of the pan with a wooden spoon.

• Add the Worcestershire sauce, potatoes, bay leaves, thyme, cumin, and tomatoes. Bring the pot to a boil, then reduce to a simmer and cook for 1 hour, stirring occasionally. Add the celery, carrots, peas, rosemary, and parsley. Season to taste with salt and pepper and cook for another 30 minutes. Ladle into soup bowls and serve.

THE SIMPLE PLEASURES
OF BREAD AND SOUP

The earliest breads were simple, flat cakes, a form still popular in many cuisines today. Yeast breads made their debut about nine thousand years ago in Sumaria and were probably created by accident when dough was left unattended long enough to allow the fermentation caused by yeast to begin. The process of leavening was perfected centuries later when the oven was invented in Egypt, giving rise to a whole new world of texture and flavor.

Bread had its beginnings in America even before shiploads of wheat arrived on these shores. Native Americans gave the recipe for cornbread to the European settlers, whose early wheat crops failed on the East Coast. The new Americans gradually found better growing conditions for wheat as they edged westward, and by the time the Revolutionary War cut off many European supplies, wheat had grown to become America's leading crop.

The rich farmlands tilled by the Pennsylvania Dutch near Philadelphia supplied much of the wheat that sustained Revolutionary troops in their encampments around the Delaware River. American wheat crops were as successful as George Washington's army, and by the time the war ended in 1776, 75 tons of wheat from Washington's farm alone had been shipped overseas, generating trade that would continue to build to this day.

The European tradition of town bakers gave way in America to home-baked bread, especially as pioneers forged westward and population was spread thin. As late as the beginning of this century, 95 percent of all flour sold in this country was purchased to bake homemade bread, and the perfume of loaves in the oven wafted out of kitchen windows across the land. As cities and industry grew, people began working more and baking less. Commercially made bread became a mainstay in most homes. Hours were recaptured, but lost were the flavor and aroma of bread fresh from the oven.

Yet as with many other traditions, bread made by hand is enjoying a comeback. Today, Americans are re-experiencing the joy of what James Beard called "the most fundamentally satisfying of all foods" by taking the time to enjoy the process of making bread at home and by patronizing local bakeries that sell bread fresh from their ovens. Simple meals such as bread and homemade soup recall the wholesome repasts that sustained our forefathers and mothers and reclaim for today's harried diners the basic pleasures of home and hearth.

MORSEL

Yeast

Something alive lurks in the pantry of every baker, and it comes out only to work its magic in the oven. Yeast is a single-celled microscopic organism that, as it grows, converts food into alcohol and carbon dioxide in a process called fermentation. Yeast thrives on moisture, food in the form of sugar or starch, and warm temperatures. Given the right conditions, the carbon dioxide it produces causes bread dough to rise, which in turn creates the airy loaves that make our mouths water.

Baker's yeast is available in three forms: active dry yeast, compressed fresh yeast, and yeast starters. The tiny, dehydrated granules that form active dry yeast are available in 1/4-ounce packets for single recipes or in jars for those who do a lot of baking. Although it is alive, this dry yeast is dormant until it is revived with warm liquid. This form of yeast has a relatively long shelf life and is reliable up until the date stamped on the package.

Unlike active dry yeast, the small squares of compressed fresh yeast are very perishable and must be kept refrigerated and used within a week or two. One cake of fresh yeast and a packet of dry yeast are interchangeable in most recipes. Many modern cooks rely on the more convenient dry variety, but some bakers prefer the particular quality fresh yeast gives to bread.

Yeast starters, such as those for sourdough breads, are the grandfathers of modern baking powders and yeast products. Before commercial leavening agents were on the market, homemade yeast starters were the pride of every baker. Early bread makers relied on airborne yeast to create starters by activating mixtures of flour, water, and sugar. Once the fermentation process is complete, part of the starter can be reserved for future baking and supplemented by continually adding flour and water. Starters are often regarded as a baker's secret ingredient and are carefully nurtured and guarded in the deep recesses of the kitchen.

LE BUS SESAME SEMOLINA

This recipe for bread comes from David Braverman, whose instincts for quality and creativity are quite apparent in the oven-fresh goods made in his Philadelphia bakery, Le Bus. He chose the baking profession because he enjoys the challenge involved in bread chemistry, the sensuous experience of feeling the dough and smelling the bread as it bakes, and of course, tasting the final product.

Ingredients for the Biga (starter)

1/4 ounce dry active yeast or one cake fresh yeast

1 1/2 cups water, at room temperature (70°F)

3 cups bread flour

1/2 teaspoon salt

Ingredients for the Dough

1 recipe for biga (see above)

1 1/2 pounds water (at 60°F)

1/4 ounce fresh yeast

2 tablespoons malt syrup (optional)

1 pound semolina flour

1 pound bread flour

2 tablespoons salt

sesame seeds

Method

· To make the biga, dissolve the yeast in the water for several minutes. Mix the flour and salt together in a bowl, then blend in the yeast with a spoon until combined. Turn the mixture onto a lightly floured worktable and knead briefly, until a ball is formed. It will be rough and fairly stiff. Place the biga in a lightly oiled bowl, cover with plastic wrap, and refrigerate for 24 hours.

· Preheat the oven to 375°F.

· To make the dough, remove the biga from the refrigerator and cut it into small pieces. Place it in the bowl of a heavy-duty electric mixer and add the water, yeast, and malt syrup. Blend on low speed briefly to begin to slightly dissolve the biga.

· Turn the mixer off and add the semolina and bread flours. Mix on low speed until all the flour is incorporated. Increase the speed to medium and mix for 7 to 10 minutes, until a smooth dough is achieved. The temperature of the dough should be about 75°F.

· Remove the dough and turn it into a lightly oiled bowl. Cover the bowl and allow the dough to rise for 1 1/2 to 2 hours, until doubled in size. Punch the dough down, turn onto a floured work surface, and cut into 5-ounce rolls or 1-pound loaves. Roll gently into rounds and allow to rest for 20 minutes.

· Reshape into rolls or loaves as desired. Allow the dough to rise a final time on boards dusted with cornmeal for 1 to 1 1/2 hours, or until two-thirds risen. Sprinkle with sesame seeds and slash the tops with a sharp knife. Bake for 35 to 40 minutes.

VEGETABLE SOUP WITH VEAL MEATBALLS

4 servings

Ingredients

2 quarts chicken stock or broth

2 tablespoons European-style butter
(such as Keller's)

1 tablespoon fresh garlic, minced

2 medium onions, diced

2 celery stalks, diced

1 medium carrot, peeled and diced

1 parsnip, peeled and diced

2 tablespoons tomato purée

1/2 large acorn squash, peeled, seeded, and diced

1 thick slice crusty French or Italian bread

3 small, whole cloves garlic

2 eggs

12 ounces raw, boneless veal, trimmed of fat

2 ounces smoked ham, coarsely diced

freshly ground black pepper

1/4 teaspoon dried basil

1/4 teaspoon dried oregano

unbleached all-purpose flour

salt to taste

Method

• Bring the chicken stock or broth to a boil in a large soup pot. Turn the heat to medium-low and allow to simmer, uncovered, while you continue.

• Heat the butter in a skillet over medium heat. Add the garlic and onions and sauté for 2 to 3 minutes. Add the celery, carrot, and parsnip and sauté for another 5 minutes. Add the sautéed vegetables, tomato purée, and squash to the simmering stock. Cover and let simmer gently for about 15 minutes.

• Combine the bread, garlic, and eggs in a food processor for about 30 seconds, until a smooth paste is formed. Add the veal, ham, pepper, basil, and oregano. Pulse 10 to 15 times or until a smooth, very thick paste is formed. Remove the paste from the processor and form it into balls the size of large marbles. Roll the balls in the flour until lightly dusted.

• When vegetables are tender, raise the heat so that the soup simmers a little more intensely. Drop the meatballs into the soup and cook for 5 to 7 minutes. Add salt and adjust the seasoning, ladle into soup bowls, and serve with slices of homemade bread.

BREAD PUDDING WITH KEY LIME SAUCE AND CHANTILLY CREAM

4 to 6 servings

Ingredients

2 cups milk

4 eggs

1 1/4 cups plus 1 tablespoon sugar

6 tablespoons melted European-style butter (such as Keller's)

1/2 teaspoon vanilla extract

1 teaspoon cinnamon

1/4 teaspoon nutmeg

3 ounces French bread (1/2 of a baguette), cut into 1-inch pieces

1/2 cup chopped walnuts

3/4 cup currants

1 tablespoon cornstarch

1/4 cup plus 3 tablespoons water

1/2 cup Key lime juice (any lime juice can be used if Key limes are unavailable)

Chantilly Cream (recipe on page 12)

Method

• Preheat the oven to 350°F.

• In a large bowl, whisk together the milk, eggs, 3/4 cup of the sugar, the melted butter, vanilla, cinnamon, and nutmeg until the sugar dissolves. Add the bread and set aside. Stir occasionally for about 30 minutes, until the bread is soft.

• Stir the walnut pieces and currants into the softened bread and pour the mixture into a buttered 2-quart baking dish. Cover with foil and place the dish in a large roasting pan. Add enough warm water to reach halfway up the sides of the baking dish. Bake for 30 minutes, remove the foil, and continue to bake until the pudding is set in the middle (about 20 minutes).

• In a small bowl, dissolve the cornstarch in 3 tablespoons water. In a small non-aluminum saucepan, stir together the remaining 1/2 cup plus 1 tablespoon sugar, the lime juice, and the remaining 1/4 cup water. Bring to a boil over moderate heat to dissolve the sugar. Stir in the cornstarch mixture and boil, stirring, for about 30 seconds, or until the lime sauce thickens.

• To serve, spread 2 to 3 tablespoons of lime sauce on each plate. Scoop the warm pudding onto the sauce and top off with Chantilly Cream.

CHEF'S TIP:
Florida produces the famous variety of limes named for the tropical Keys of the state. Key limes are smaller, rounder, and more yellow than Persian limes, which are the variety most often found in supermarkets. Specialty food stores often feature Key limes in summer, their peak season.

CHANTILLY CREAM

Ingredients

1 cup heavy cream, chilled

1/2 cup sour cream

1 tablespoon sugar

1 tablespoon brandy

1/2 teaspoon vanilla extract

Method

- Combine all the ingredients in a mixing bowl and beat until thick, about 2 to 5 minutes.

EAT YOUR VEGETABLES

Once relegated to the edge of the plate and served just for contrast to the entrée, vegetables are now headline news and the darlings of chefs as well as nutritionists. Restaurants are whittling meat servings to healthier proportions and allowing generous helpings of vegetables to share center stage on plates. Vegetarian dishes that used to be shunned by our somewhat carnivorous society are now embraced by a wide variety of people. Vegetables are finally getting the attention they deserve, but this is not their first brush with stardom.

The current most-favored status of vegetables mirrors our earliest relationship with these healthy foods. Ever since prehistoric cultures supplemented any meat they acquired with the plants that grew around them, vegetables have played an important role in the human diet. Agriculture was born from the need to increase the availability of these natural resources, and people have been trying to improve the system from the time the first seeds were cultivated.

At first, people only ate vegetables indigenous to their homeland. Historic events such as the expansion of the Roman Empire, the Crusades, and the discovery of the New World made agricultural products from around the globe available to all cultures. Meanwhile, farmers began to tinker with genetics by carefully choosing the hardiest and fastest-growing plants to reseed their fields. This early selective horticulture paved the way for the emerging agricultural industry.

Large quantities of vegetables and fruits were shipped around the world during the early days of the food trade, but their availability was limited by the length of time they were in season and how long they lasted in transit. In the first part of the twentieth century, the flash-freezing technique created by Clarence Birdseye, combined with refrigerated railroad cars (invented, ironically, by meat tycoon Gustave Swift), offered consumers a constant harvest. The canning industry, perfected in France in the 1920s, increased product reliability. Yet this modern efficiency was not without cost. Vegetables lost their garden-fresh flavor, and people lost interest in vegetables.

Produce was welcomed back to the table after a few modern trends made the most of what these foods could offer. Air freight provided swift transit for a wide variety of fresh vegetables from field to market. The resurgence of American regional cuisines celebrates the bounty of each area by emphasizing local vegetables in season. Finally, the tendency to overcook and generously sauce vegetables has given way to letting them shine on their own, with a minimum of flavor enhancement. These innovations, which coincided with the trend toward healthier eating, made vegetables ripe to rise to the top of the culinary A-list once again.

MORSEL

Asparagus

The exact origin of asparagus is unknown, but historical records show that the ancient Romans and Greeks were equally impressed with the tasty stalks growing wild in the hills surrounding the Mediterranean Sea. Julius Caesar is noted to be among the first to prefer his asparagus served with melted butter. Emperor Augustus ordered his kitchen to cook asparagus only briefly, thereby setting the standard for preparing the vegetable today and inspiring the phrase "faster than you can cook asparagus," the Roman equivalent of "quicker than a New York minute."

The Egyptians were the first to cultivate this member of the lily family over two thousand years ago, and were so taken with its value that they sacrificed bundles of the stalks to their gods. The first asparagus grown in hotbeds appeared in the gardens of Louis XIV, whose horticulturist was ordered to provide a year-round supply of the vegetable for the king...not for its flavor, but because it was considered an aphrodisiac.

MORSEL

Shallots

Shallots are the more delicate and sophisticated cousins of onions and garlic, although if need be, these three members of the lily family can be substituted for one another (in varying proportions) in recipes. When first mentioned in print in English, shallots were also referred to as Spanish garlic. Actually, they are native to central Asia and were enthusiastically used by the Romans, who introduced them to the rest of their empire. Shallots found their way into the hearts of European chefs as their different cuisines developed, then they crossed the Atlantic to enhance the melting pot of ethnic foods we enjoy in this country. Today, most American shallots are produced in New Jersey and New York.

GARDEN VEGETABLE SALAD WITH ROASTED SHALLOT VINAIGRETTE

4 servings

Ingredients

3 whole shallots, peeled and quartered

3/4 cup olive oil

1/2 teaspoon sugar

salt and freshly ground black pepper to taste

1/4 pound fresh baby green beans (haricots verts)

1/3 cup white wine vinegar

2 small heads Bibb lettuce, washed

1 pint red cherry tomatoes, cut into halves

3 ears of fresh corn, kernels cut from the cob

1/2 red pepper, sliced julienne
(see Chef's Tip)

Method

• Preheat the oven to 350°F.

• Combine the shallots, olive oil, sugar, salt, and pepper in a shallow baking pan. Roast in the oven for about 20 to 30 minutes, or until the shallots are soft. Remove the shallots from the pan and allow to cool. Reserve the oil.

• Blanch and chill the green beans.

• Place the shallots in a food processor, add the vinegar, and pulse to combine. Slowly add the reserved oil and process until an emulsion is formed.

• Cut 1 head of the Bibb lettuce into chiffonade (see Chef's Tip, below). Separate the leaves from the other head and leave them whole. Arrange the whole lettuce leaves in the center of 4 plates. Place the green beans around the lettuce so that they fan outward.

• In a bowl, toss the chiffonade lettuce, tomatoes, and corn with the vinaigrette and place on top of the whole lettuce leaves. Garnish the salads with the red pepper.

CHEF'S TIP:

Julienne is a French culinary term for foods that have been finely shredded or cut into matchstick-length strips, as in the recipe above. It is also the name of a clear soup or consommé to which shredded vegetables have been added. The term was coined in the seventeenth century, and the delicate-looking preparation was probably given its name in honor of a favorite lady.

The French also gave us the word *chiffonade*, which translates to "made of rags." It is actually an elegant-looking preparation in which vegetables, usually lettuces, are sliced into long, thin shreds.

SUMMER VEGETABLE RISOTTO

4 to 6 servings

Ingredients

6 cups tomato juice

2 cups water

1/4 teaspoon saffron

3 tablespoons European-style butter
(such as Keller's)

1 small red onion, finely chopped

1 tablespoon chopped fresh garlic

2 cups Arborio rice (a high-starch Italian variety,
available in most markets)

1 bunch asparagus, cut into 1-inch pieces

1 tomato, seeded and diced

1 cup fresh peas

1/2 cup fresh scallions, chopped

1 small green pepper, diced

1 small yellow pepper, diced

3/4 cup grated Parmesan cheese

1 1/2 tablespoons fresh basil

salt and pepper to taste

Method

• Bring the tomato juice and water to a boil in a saucepan. Add the saffron.

• Melt the butter in another saucepan and add the onion and garlic. Sauté until the onion is translucent. Add the rice and stir for 2 minutes. Add the tomato broth 1/2 cup at a time, stirring constantly until each addition is absorbed before adding the next.

• Add the vegetables just before the last addition of liquid. When all the liquid has been absorbed, add the Parmesan cheese, basil, and salt and pepper. Cover and let rest for several minutes before serving.

PEAR AND SUN-DRIED CHERRY COBBLER

6 servings

Ingredients for the Filling

1 cup cranberry juice

1 cup sun-dried tart cherries

6 Bartlett pears

3/4 cup light brown sugar

1/2 teaspoon cinnamon

1/2 teaspoon cornstarch

Ingredients for the Topping

1 cup all-purpose flour

1/4 teaspoon baking powder

3/4 cup sugar

1 egg

1 cup milk

1 teaspoon vanilla

1/2 teaspoon lemon zest

Method for the Filling

- Warm the cranberry juice in a saucepan and add the cherries. Simmer for a few minutes to allow the cherries to reconstitute. Remove the pan from the stove and drain the cherries, discarding the juice.

- Peel, core, and dice the pears. Combine the pears, brown sugar, cinnamon, cornstarch, and cherries in a bowl and mix thoroughly. Divide the cobbler filling among 6 individual buttered and sugared ramekins.

Method for the Topping

- Preheat the oven to 350°F.

- Sift the flour and baking powder together into a bowl. Add the sugar, egg, milk, vanilla, and lemon zest. Beat together just until combined. Pour the batter evenly over the filling and bake the cobblers for about 15 to 20 minutes, or until golden brown.

TRISH MORRISSEY

— Philadelphia Fish & Company —

Trish Morrissey is a Pennsylvania native, but she spent the first twelve years of her life living in Panama, Italy, and Germany. After graduating from Drexel University in Philadelphia, she experimented with professional cooking and soon set aside her degree in fashion and merchandising to become a chef.

Morrissey attended The Restaurant School of Philadelphia, completing an associate's degree in culinary arts in 1995. Throughout culinary school she apprenticed at the Ritz-Carlton Hotel in Philadelphia as a pastry chef. After graduation, she became a full-time employee at the hotel and worked her way up to become the Ritz-Carlton's first female dining room chef. Under her leadership, the Dining Room was awarded the Dirona award and was named by *Gourmet* magazine as one of Philadelphia's "top 20 tables" in 1996 and 1997.

In 1997, Morrissey was the recipient of the Panache award, which is presented to women of achievement in the hospitality field by the Philadelphia Delaware Valley Restaurant Association. That year she was also inducted into the Philadelphia chapter of the international women's culinary organization Les Dames d'Escoffier. Her earliest cooking influences were her mother and grandmother, who both taught her about Italian comfort food and gave her an appreciation for fresh ingredients and home cooking. Now, as executive chef at Philadelphia Fish & Company, Morrissey is "finding true pleasure in creating perfect basics with a twist."

MORSEL

Salmon

When European settlers arrived in America, they were overwhelmed with the number of Atlantic salmon that spawned seasonally in rivers up and down the East Coast. The plentiful fish, which had long been a dependable source of nutrition for Native Americans, became a colonial staple. Salmon was often served three times a day, and it began to draw the same dull response the Thanksgiving turkey gets after days of leftovers. It was so easily obtained and served so frequently that a clause was inserted in the contracts of indentured servants limiting their rations of salmon to no more than once a week!

By 1889, catches of Atlantic salmon in Maine alone surpassed 150,000 pounds. In 1950, the same waters produced only about eighty-two of the fish. Like other species of fish that depend upon freshwater streams for spawning, salmon fell victim to overfishing, pollution, and the damming of American rivers. Today, about 70 percent of the salmon brought to market is harvested through aquaculture, and strict standards govern the management of remaining wild fish stocks. Plentiful supplies of non-endangered salmon are now sold at markets across the country, making it one of the most inexpensive and popular ways to incorporate nutritious fish into the American diet.

VIDALIA ONION VICHYSSOISE WITH SMOKED SALMON

4 to 6 servings

Ingredients for the Vichyssoise

2 tablespoons unsalted butter

2 Vidalia (or other large, sweet) onions, sliced

2 Idaho potatoes, peeled and roughly chopped

1 quart chicken or vegetable stock, defatted

1 1/2 cups crème fraîche or heavy cream

salt and white pepper to taste

Ingredients for the Garnish

4 ounces smoked salmon, sliced into thin strips

2 tablespoons crème fraîche, or heavy cream, whipped

caviar (optional)

4 sprigs chervil

Method

- Melt the butter in a large pot and add the onions. Cook the onions until caramelized (brown, but not burned). Add the potatoes and the chicken or vegetable stock and simmer for 45 minutes.

- Let the mixture cool, then purée the soup. Pass the soup through a sieve. Add the crème fraîche or cream and season with salt and pepper.

- Serve the soup in shallow bowls. In the center of each bowl, place salmon strips, dollops of crème fraîche or whipped cream, and caviar. Finish with sprigs of chervil.

CIDER BARBECUE SALMON

6 servings

Ingredients

6 8-ounce salmon fillets

salt and pepper to taste

nonstick cooking spray

Cider Barbecue Sauce (recipe follows)

Nutty Apple and Blue Cheese Mashed Potatoes (recipe on page 23)

Method

- Heat a broiler pan or outdoor grill over medium-high heat. (If using a broiler pan, preheat the oven to 350°F.) Season each fillet with salt and pepper, then spray with cooking spray. Place the fillets on the broiler pan under a broiler, or place them directly on the grill.

- After 2 minutes, turn each fillet 1/4 turn. After 2 more minutes, turn them over and cook for an additional 2 minutes.

- If using a broiler pan, put the salmon on a sheet pan and drizzle each fillet with 2 tablespoons Cider Barbecue Sauce. Cook for 5 to 8 minutes, to taste.

- If using an outdoor grill, top each fillet with 2 tablespoons Cider Barbecue Sauce. Cover the grill and cook to taste. Serve over Nutty Apple and Blue Cheese Mashed Potatoes and drizzle the remaining Cider Barbecue Sauce over each plate.

CIDER BARBECUE SAUCE

3 cups

Ingredients

2 tablespoons butter

1 medium onion, finely diced

2 tablespoons dark molasses

2 tablespoons Worcestershire sauce

3 cups apple cider vinegar

3 tablespoons tomato paste

1/2 teaspoon chili powder

1/2 teaspoon cinnamon

1/2 teaspoon salt

Method

- In a medium-size saucepan, melt the butter over medium heat. Add the onion and sauté for 4 to 5 minutes, until soft. Add the rest of the ingredients. Mix well and simmer on low heat for 30 minutes, stirring frequently. Serve warm or cool; refrigerate any unused portion.

Curried Acorn Squash Soup, page 145

Steamed Mussels with Wine and Herbs, page 61

Callaloo Tart, page 101

Chilled Grilled Black Mission Figs with Virginia Country Ham and Lime Cream, page 167

Garden Vegetable Salad with Roasted Shallot Vinaigrette, page 15

Home-Style Chicken Soup, page 107

Tomato Onion Sesame Biscuits, page 31

NUTTY APPLE AND BLUE CHEESE MASHED POTATOES

4 to 6 servings

Ingredients

2 Granny Smith apples, peeled, cored, and quartered

1 tablespoon brown sugar

1 tablespoon oil

2 pounds Idaho potatoes, peeled and quartered

1 teaspoon salt

8 tablespoons unsalted butter

1/2 cup heavy cream

1/2 cup milk

1/2 cup chopped toasted walnuts

1/2 cup crumbled blue cheese

salt and white pepper to taste

Method

- Preheat the oven to 375°F.

- Toss the apples with the brown sugar and oil. Bake the apples in the oven for 20 minutes, or until tender but not mushy. Remove from the oven and allow to cool. Dice the apples into 1/4-inch pieces and set aside.

- Place the potatoes in a 2-quart saucepan with 1 teaspoon salt and enough cold water to cover. Cover the pan and bring the water to a boil, then lower the heat and simmer until tender, about 30 minutes. Test the potatoes by piercing them with a knife. (It should slide in easily.) Place the potatoes in a strainer and drain well.

- Combine the butter, cream, and milk in another saucepan and heat until the butter has melted. Keep warm.

- Working over the saucepan used to cook the potatoes, pass the potatoes through a food mill or potato ricer. Put the pan on the stove over low heat and begin adding the warm cream mixture. Be certain to mix well with a wooden spoon. After adding all the liquid, fold in the apples, nuts, and blue cheese. Season with salt and white pepper. Serve at once or keep warm in the top half of a covered double boiler over simmering water.

CRANBERRY WATER ICE AND CREAM

4 to 6 servings

Ingredients

1 1/2 cups cranberry sauce

2 cups ice-cold water

zest of 1 lemon

juice of 1 lemon

2 cups vanilla ice cream

6 thick pretzel rods

Method

• In a medium-size saucepan, heat the cranberry sauce over low heat, stirring constantly until melted. Remove from the heat and stir in the water, lemon zest, and lemon juice. Refrigerate until chilled.

• Pour the cranberry mixture into a 9 x 9-inch shallow baking pan covered with foil. Freeze until firm, about 3 hours. Place the bowl and blade of a food processor in the freezer. When they are chilled, remove them and the cranberry ice from the freezer. Process the cranberry ice until it is fluffy, then return it to the pan and cover. Freeze until firm.

• Run the ice through a food processor again, and refreeze. In a parfait or pilsner glass, layer cranberry water ice and ice cream and garnish with the pretzel rods.

A TASTE OF CHESAPEAKE BAY

When Captain John Smith first sailed into the waters of Chesapeake Bay in 1608, he and his crewmen were overwhelmed with the bounty that the waterway and its surrounding landscape had to offer. As the Native Americans had discovered long before, the river teemed with fish and shellfish, and the moderate weather provided first the gatherer and later the farmer with rich rewards. A wide variety of wild game thrived in the region, and when Europeans settled there, their farm animals reveled in lush pastures. It is not surprising that one of America's earliest and most satisfying regional cuisines was born on the Chesapeake Bay.

As any Eastern Shore native will tell you, the area's trademark foods are so delicious that they are best served at their simplest. Recipes for crab cakes or grilled oysters contain just enough seasoning to allow the seafood to shine. Shellfish are often merely steamed with a few herbs and spices, and fish are presented hot off the grill, brushed only with lemon butter. Condiments and side dishes are chosen to complement rather than compete with this basic cooking style.

Timing is everything in kitchens on the Chesapeake Bay. The seafood must be from a recent catch, and crabs and shellfish have to be kept alive until they are cooked. Produce cannot be anything but farm fresh. Colonial cooks began the Chesapeake tradition of single-pot meals, each of which offers a sampler of the freshest and best the region has to offer. Delicacies ranging from freshly picked corn and new potatoes to clams and crabs right out of the bay, plus local sausage or other meats, are added to the pot in sequence so each item is cooked just right.

The Latin name for blue crab means "beautiful swimmers," and these crustaceans are indeed beautiful to the economy and cuisine of the region. According to many, they are what have made the Chesapeake Bay famous. In the crab houses that line the bay, experienced "pickers" remove the tasty steamed meat for commercial sale. They process about half the blue crabs caught each season, and the rest are sold live to cook at home or in restaurants. Chesapeake residents cherish their backyard crab fests, and the shore's crab shacks, where patrons dine over newspaper on all the crab they can eat, are legendary.

Along with the mouthwatering flavors of the cuisine, visitors to the Chesapeake Bay will remember the straightforward, friendly people who are openly grateful for their surroundings and work together to preserve their unique environment. The Chesapeake Bay Foundation was created to combat the pollution, overfishing, and loss of wetlands that have threatened this area in recent years. Through the conservation efforts of the Chesapeake Bay Foundation, the bay will endure as "the land of pleasant living" by those who call it home.

MORSEL

Soft-Shell Crabs

Soft-shell crabs are not a separate species of crab; they are just a growth phase in the life cycle of blue crabs. Their shells gradually become too tight as they grow, so the crabs molt out of their snug armor and grow roomier protection. When the old shell is discarded, a crab is considered a "soft-shell" for the seventy-two hours before its new shell hardens. It is during this brief time span that soft-shell crabs must be harvested and sold.

Skilled watermen on the Chesapeake can predict when crabs are about to shed their shells, and they gather them in holding tanks to await their metamorphosis. When their moment arrives, the crabs are marketed live or flash-frozen to be shipped across the country. Every part of a soft-shell crab is edible; they are usually sautéed or deep-fried whole.

SOFT-SHELL CRAB AND SWEET CORN CHOWDER

4 to 6 servings

Ingredients

3 strips raw bacon, sliced

1/2 small onion, thinly sliced

1 teaspoon chopped garlic

1 celery stalk, diced

1 1/2 cups clam juice

1/2 cup chicken stock

2 cups whole milk

1/2 teaspoon dried thyme

1/2 teaspoon dried oregano

1 bay leaf

1 potato, peeled and diced

1 cup fresh corn kernels

3 soft-shell crabs, cleaned and cut into bite-size pieces

1 tablespoon cornstarch

1 tablespoon water

salt and pepper to taste

Method

· In a soup pot, cook the bacon until the fat melts, then add the onion, garlic, and celery. Sauté for 3 to 5 minutes.

· Pour in the clam juice, chicken stock, and milk. Add the thyme, oregano, and bay leaf and bring to a boil. Add the potato and simmer, covered, until the potato pieces are barely tender. Stir in the corn and cook for another 5 minutes.

· Add the soft-shell crabs and simmer for another 3 to 5 minutes. Add the cornstarch to the water and thicken the soup with the cornstarch mixture, stirring well. Season with salt and pepper. Ladle into soup bowls and serve.

A TRADITIONAL CHESAPEAKE CRAB BAKE

4 to 6 servings

Ingredients

12 very small new potatoes, washed

4 large blueclaw crabs

2 tablespoons Old Bay Seasoning

4 ears of corn, husks and silks removed

24 littleneck clams, scrubbed

4 4-ounce kielbasa sausages

16 mussels, scrubbed, beards removed

16 tablespoons (2 sticks) unsalted European-style butter (such as Keller's), melted

2 lemons, cut into wedges

Method

• Fill two pots, large enough to hold 2 bamboo steamers each, with 2 to 4 inches of water. Bring the water to a boil in both pots.

• Place the potatoes in a steamer on the bottom of the first pot and the crabs, seasoned with the Old Bay, in another steamer placed on top of the first in the same pot.

• Begin the second set of bamboo steamers after the first has cooked for about 5 to 7 minutes. Put the corn in the bottom steamer of the second pot. Put the clams and kielbasa in the top steamer and cook for about 5 minutes.

• After 5 minutes, add the mussels to the steamer basket containing the clams and kielbasa and continue to cook for about another 5 minutes. While the seafood is cooking, melt the butter and keep it warm.

• Both steamer pots should be done at the same time, after about 15 to 20 minutes, or when all the seafood is cooked. Serve everything on large platters with melted butter and lemon wedges.

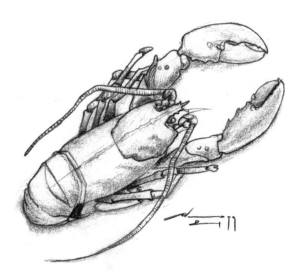

WHISKEY CHOCOLATE PECAN PIE

8 servings

Ingredients

6 tablespoons European-style butter
(such as Keller's)

3 eggs, beaten

1 cup sugar

1 cup dark corn syrup

1 tablespoon flour

1 teaspoon vanilla extract

3 ounces unsweetened chocolate,
melted and cooled to room temperature

1/4 cup bourbon

1   9-inch pie shell

1 1/2 cups pecan halves

fresh mint, for garnish

Method

- Preheat the oven to 400°F.

- Melt the butter and allow it to cool to room temperature. Beat the eggs with the sugar in a large bowl. Stir in the corn syrup, melted butter, flour, vanilla, chocolate, and bourbon.

- Pour the mixture into the pie shell and top with the pecan halves. Bake in the oven for 20 minutes, then reduce the heat to 325°F and bake for an additional 25 to 30 minutes, or until a knife inserted in the pie comes out clean.

- Remove the pie from the oven and set it on a wire rack to cool. Slice and serve garnished with the fresh mint.

ASHBELL McELVEEN

— Cyberchef —

Ashbell McElveen has traveled thousands of miles to gather information about regional cuisines from around the world, which he shares on television shows, videos, and his own Web site. Originally from South Carolina, he first became interested in international culinary traditions while studying cooking in France. He went on to explore the foods of Africa and Asia and developed a reputation for his extensive multicultural culinary knowledge.

McElveen is frequently seen on television and from 1993 to 1995 hosted a culinary segment on the Sunday *Today* show. Some of his more popular pieces included a Hispanic celebration of Christmas that featured a roast suckling pig and an octopus salad and a fried chicken tribute to his literary neighbor, Ralph Ellison.

In 1995, McElveen established his own Web site, Foodstop (www.foodstop.com), where he is known as Chef Ashbell and dispenses information about world cuisines. Foodstop has been highly recommended by *Net Guide* and was chosen "the best byte of food" by *HotWired* magazine in 1996. McElveen still travels extensively in pursuit of interesting foods, flavors, and culinary traditions and trends around the world.

MORSEL

Sweet Potatoes vs. Yams

Sweet potatoes and yams are not the same food, despite what many people think. They are not even botanical kin, and they originated on opposite sides of the planet. The sweet potato plant is a South American native and a member of the morning glory family, with which it shares delicate blossoms and wandering vines. Yams, which are tubers, got their start in Africa and tropical Asia from a plant related to grasses and lilies. Assumptions about the shared identity of these vegetables began when both plants were discovered at about the same time by European explorers.

Portuguese traders found large, strange roots in Africa and called them yams, which was a version of an African name for the food. They brought them back to Europe, where they were sampled as curiosities. Christopher Columbus' familiarity with the yam caused him to misidentify the sweet potatoes he was served when he landed in St. Thomas. He called them batatas, *from the Native American word for sweet potatoes, and shipped them back home. In English, the word became "potatoes," and soon Europeans were using that term for both types of imported tubers, adding the "sweet" when white potatoes arrived in the Old World.*

While yams were being called sweet potatoes in Europe, in the colonies sweet potatoes were dubbed "yams" by African slaves, who mistook them for their native food. The misconception about the two tubers persists, and even food suppliers frequently assign the name "yam" to one of the two types of sweet potato sold in the United States. Actually, true yams are not cultivated in this country; they are imported only in small numbers and are sold in ethnic markets, rarely in supermarkets.

TOMATO ONION SESAME BISCUITS

6 to 8 servings

Ingredients

2 cups all-purpose flour

1/2 teaspoon salt

1/2 teaspoon sugar

2 teaspoons baking powder

1 stick cold butter, cut into small pieces

1 cup buttermilk (slightly more may be needed)

2 firm, ripe tomatoes, cut into 1/16-inch slices

2 medium white onions, cut into 1/16-inch slices

1 cup sesame seeds

1 cup cream cheese

Method

- Preheat the oven to 450°F.

- Sift the flour, salt, sugar, and baking powder together in a bowl. Using two forks or a pastry cutter, cut in the butter until you get the consistency of coarse meal (do not use your hands, which will melt the butter). Do not overmix.

- Add enough buttermilk to form a ball of dough. Turn the dough out onto a floured board and knead twice. Roll out the dough to 1/4 inch thick and cut out circles with a teacup or a biscuit cutter. Place the biscuits on a greased cookie sheet. Place a slice of tomato and onion on each biscuit. Dot with butter and top with sesame seeds.

- Bake for 15 minutes, or until golden brown. Top with a little cream cheese and serve hot.

SEA ISLAND SMOTHERED SHRIMP OVER FRIED GRITS

6 s e r v i n g s

Ingredients for the Shrimp

1 tablespoon cold, sweet butter

1 teaspoon fresh thyme

1 medium onion, thinly sliced

2 red bell peppers, sliced julienne

2 teaspoons peanut oil

2 pounds large shrimp, peeled and deveined

salt and pepper to taste

all-purpose flour, for dredging

2 cups shrimp stock (To make, simmer the shrimp shells with 1 small onion and 1 quart of water for 1 hour and then strain; boil to reduce to 2 cups of liquid. Or you can use chicken stock.)

1/4 cup sherry

1 bunch fresh chives

Ingredients for the Fried Grits

1 quart milk

1 tablespoon butter

1 scallion (keep whole)

4 cups stone-ground yellow grits

salt to taste

peanut oil, for frying

1 egg, beaten

breadcrumbs, for dredging

Method for the Shrimp

- In a skillet, heat 1/2 tablespoon of the butter and sauté the thyme for 30 seconds. Add the onion and bell peppers; cook until wilted, about 5 minutes. Set aside.

- In another skillet, heat the peanut oil over medium-high heat. Season the shrimp with salt and pepper and dredge them in the flour, shaking off the excess. Pan-sear the shrimp for 2 minutes on each side, then place them in the skillet containing the vegetables. Add the shrimp stock and sherry and simmer for 15 minutes. Add the rest of the butter and the chives and mix until the butter has melted.

Method for the Fried Grits

- In a saucepan, combine the milk, butter, and scallion and bring to a boil. Slowly stir in the grits with a whisk, taking care not to get any lumps. Turn heat to low, add salt to taste, and stir constantly for the first 3 to 5 minutes. Cover and allow to simmer on low heat for 20 minutes. Discard the scallion after cooking.

- Lightly oil a glass baking dish or pan and pour in the hot grits, taking care to smooth the top. Allow the grits to come to room temperature, then cover and chill in the refrigerator for 1 hour.

- In a skillet, heat a cup of peanut oil. Cut the chilled grits into rounds with a teacup or a biscuit cutter, coat with beaten egg, and dredge in the breadcrumbs. Fry on each side until golden. Remove to a heated platter.

- To serve, arrange fried grit cakes on a plate and spoon smothered shrimp over the cakes.

SWEET POTATO PONE WITH GRAND MARNIER CREAM AND BLACKBERRIES

4 to 6 servings

Ingredients for the Pone

5 tablespoons butter

1 cup dark brown sugar

1 teaspoon freshly grated nutmeg

1/2 teaspoon finely grated ginger

1/2 cup molasses

6 cups grated sweet potatoes

zest and juice of 1 orange

pinch of salt

Method for the Pone

- In a large skillet, heat the butter, brown sugar, nutmeg, ginger, and molasses until melted. Add the grated sweet potatoes, orange zest, orange juice, and salt and allow to simmer over low heat, carefully stirring the potatoes as they cook. The object is to cook slowly, stirring the mixture until it achieves a rich brown color, about 40 minutes. The mixture will become very thick. After cooking, keep warm in the oven.

Ingredients for the Sauce

2 1/2 cups heavy cream

1 teaspoon butter

1 teaspoon orange zest

1/2 cup Grand Marnier liqueur

fresh blackberries, for garnish

Method for the Sauce

- In a saucepan, reduce the cream by almost half; add the butter and orange zest. Remove from the heat and add the Grand Marnier. Serve warm over the sweet potato pones, garnished with fresh blackberries.

COOKING WITH BEER

We're in the midst of a beer renaissance. Microbreweries are popping up from coast to coast, and the country is awash in boutique lagers, stouts, and ales. After decades of having to choose from taste-alike beers produced by a handful of giant beer companies, small breweries with distinctive products are turning Americans into beer connoisseurs.

However current the trend, this is not the first time a diversity of brews has been available in this country. In fact, Americans were making all sorts of beer from the time they stepped off the *Mayflower* onto the soil they would call home. Devotees of bottled spring water might be surprised to learn that beer was the beverage of choice in Plymouth and all other colonial settlements because local water was considered unsafe. Just as in Europe, where streams and wells were suspected of harboring germs, Americans either boiled water to drink or shunned it altogether. Beer, boiled during brewing and containing antiseptic alcohol, was considered a healthful alternative.

American settlers planted European barley and hops, but the crops were not large enough for them to get on with the business of brewing on a wide scale. Desperate for beer, early Americans got creative. Most colonial beer was made from corn, the same food that had sustained the first settlers here. Households brewed their own beer, and when corn wasn't available, they used just about anything that was on hand: pumpkins, parsnips, molasses, and even walnut tree chips—with varying results. By the time the first shots were fired in the American Revolution, however, barley and hops were established American crops, and beer brewing had become a commercial enterprise. Philadelphia became the country's premier beer-brewing center, and it developed a reputation for a product fine enough to compete with the revered old beer houses in Europe.

Beer was always meant to be served with food, and the wide variety of brews on the market today allows for the same kind of selective pairing with dishes as does wine. Because it so beautifully brings out the flavor of food, it is also an excellent recipe ingredient. The large selection of brews gives cooks a wide choice and means that delicate dishes like fish, as well as heartier fare, can be matched with beers that complement their flavors and intensity. This new "beer cuisine" is finding its way onto menus and into home kitchens, broadening American cookery with a historical favorite.

MORSEL

Mussels

Bowls of steaming mussels have been served in Europe for centuries, but in our country this delicious mollusk was ignored by all but the birds until a few decades ago. Until the late 1970s, the only American menus featuring mussels were those in ethnic restaurants. It was through exposure to Italian and French food that Americans began to develop a passion for this shellfish, which, oddly enough, has always been available in abundant quantities on the Atlantic and Pacific coasts.

Today, all American mussels sold in restaurants and food stores are farm-raised in carefully controlled waters. Most of the mussels available in supermarkets are the shiny blue-black variety. These mollusks are relatively inexpensive and are a guiltless source of protein, as they are low in fat and calories.

Mussels should always be purchased live, stored dry in a bowl in the refrigerator, and cooked no more than a day or two later. Just before cooking, they should be rinsed in several changes of cold water and their "beards," or filaments, should be trimmed from each shell with a sharp paring knife. Mussels are then ready for any number of delicious preparations.

ALE-STEAMED MUSSELS

4 to 6 servings

Ingredients

1 tablespoon vegetable oil

1 onion, coarsely chopped

6 cloves garlic, chopped

1 12-ounce bottle of ale

2 bay leaves

1/2 red bell pepper, sliced julienne

1/2 green pepper, sliced julienne

2 plum tomatoes, diced

8 pounds mussels

1 tablespoon chopped flat-leaf parsley

1 tablespoon chopped fresh savory

2 tablespoons lemon juice

salt and pepper to taste

4 tablespoons European-style butter
(such as Keller's)

Method

- Put the vegetable oil in a large pot and sauté the onion and garlic until the onion is translucent. Add all the remaining ingredients except the butter. Place a lid on the pot and steam for about 5 to 8 minutes, or until all the mussels have opened. Discard any unopened mussels. Swirl in the butter and serve in bowls with slices of good French bread.

FOUR-ONION POT ROAST WITH BEER

6 servings

Ingredients

2 tablespoons olive oil

4- to 5-pound chuck roast, boned and tied

salt and pepper to taste

1 tablespoon dried thyme

1 tablespoon dried sage

2 large onions, peeled and thinly sliced

1 pound leeks, washed and thinly sliced

1 cup pearl onions

1 carrot, peeled and diced

1 celery stalk, diced

2 large potatoes, peeled and cut into
1 1/2-inch cubes

2 shallots, chopped

1/2 cup chopped fresh parsley

1 tablespoon molasses

1 bay leaf

2 12-ounce bottles of dark beer

2 tablespoons Dijon mustard

1 tablespoon cider vinegar

1/2 bunch scallions, chopped

Method

• In a roasting pan large enough to hold the roast, heat the olive oil over medium-high heat. Season the roast with salt, pepper, thyme, and sage. Place the roast in the pan and sear on all sides.

• Remove the roast, add all the vegetables, and sauté for about 2 minutes. Add the molasses and continue to cook for about 5 minutes, stirring to prevent burning.

• Place the roast back in the pan and add the bay leaf and the beer. Cover and cook for about 1 1/2 to 2 hours over low heat, until the meat is tender. Remove the meat and keep it warm.

• Degrease the liquid in the pan and stir in the mustard and vinegar. Reduce the liquid until it is thick enough to coat the back of a spoon. Adjust the seasoning and add the scallions. Slice the roast and serve it with the sauce and vegetables.

DAD'S GINGER BREW CAKE WITH WARM APPLES

10 to 12 servings

Ingredients

2 1/2 cups all-purpose flour

2 1/2 teaspoons powdered ginger

1 teaspoon ground cinnamon

1/2 teaspoon cloves

1/4 teaspoon allspice

1 tablespoon baking soda

1/2 teaspoon salt

1 cup unsalted European-style butter
(such as Keller's), at room temperature

1 1/4 cups packed dark brown sugar

3 large eggs, at room temperature

1 cup molasses

1/4 teaspoon vanilla

3/4 cup dark beer, flat and at room temperature

4 cooking apples

1/2 cup water

2 tablespoons sugar

2 cinnamon sticks

vanilla ice cream

Method

• Preheat the oven to 350°F. Butter and flour a 12-cup Bundt pan.

• Sift together the flour, ginger, cinnamon, cloves, allspice, baking soda, and salt. Put the butter and brown sugar in the bowl of an electric mixer and beat on high speed for 1 minute. Add the eggs one at a time and beat until each is incorporated. Add the molasses and vanilla and continue to beat for 1 more minute.

• Reduce the speed to medium and add the flour mixture a little at a time, scraping the sides of the bowl as needed. Add the beer and beat until well combined. Pour the batter into the prepared pan and tap the pan on the counter to flatten the top.

• Bake for approximately 1 hour, or until a toothpick inserted in the center comes out clean. Cool the cake in the pan on a wire rack for about 15 minutes, then turn it out onto the rack.

• Peel and core the apples and cut them into 1/2-inch cubes. Put the apples and water in a saucepan over medium-high heat. Add the sugar and stir to dissolve; bring the mixture to a low boil. Add the cinnamon sticks and lower the heat to a simmer. Cook, stirring occasionally, until the apples become very soft and the liquid thickens. Remove the cinnamon sticks and ladle apples over slices of the cake. Top with the ice cream.

RIS LACOSTE

— 1789 Restaurant —

Since 1995, Ris Lacoste has presided over the kitchen of 1789 Restaurant in the nation's capital. Her sophisticated menu of seasonal American fare has taken the reputation of the already popular historic restaurant to new heights. She specializes in bold, well-seasoned food that has not only won over local and national food critics but has also made 1789 a top dinner destination for Washingtonians and visitors from all over the world.

After dabbling in the food service industry during college, Lacoste moved to Paris to pursue her studies in French and landed a job as a receptionist and secretary at the famed cooking school La Varenne. She became interested in the classes there and emerged with a *grand diplôme* and a practical education in the French culinary scene of that period.

Before returning to the States, she spent a few months as a sous chef in France. In 1982, Lacoste cooked her first American meal at the Harvest Restaurant in Cambridge, Massachusetts, where she was hired by chef Bob Kinkead. The two went on to collaborate on several other successful ventures, including 21 Federal in Nantucket and Kinkead's in Washington, D.C., before Lacoste took over as chef at 1789.

In addition to her leadership in the kitchen, she has been active in the food world and in the community. She has served as president of the board of the Washington, D.C., chapter of the American Institute of Wine and Food since 1995, and she participates regularly in fundraising events to alleviate hunger and promote AIDS research.

Lacoste is renowned for her artistry and her passion for food, which not only delight diners but also set a striking example for young chefs in her kitchen. As one food critic noted, "In every dish she strives for a balance that keeps the whole mouth perfectly happy." Diners in her restaurant, which is rich with historical associations, sense that these are the glory days for the 1789 kitchen.

MORSEL

Capers

The caper bush is a daredevil plant that originated in what is now the Sahara Desert and managed to survive in that inhospitable environment. Today it is a prickly but beautiful bush that grows all around the Mediterranean Sea.

The Sumerians were the first to cook with the flower buds from the bush about three thousand years ago, and capers are one of the foods mentioned in the Old Testament. The ancient Greeks and Romans relished the little green buds because they added abundant flavor to bland or less-than-fresh food. By the time the great French chef Escoffier introduced modern gourmet cuisine in the 1800s, capers had earned a place of honor in many classic preparations.

There are more than 150 species of the caper shrub, and the size of the buds ranges from as small as peppercorns to as large as a fingertip. The more delicate, tiny capers are considered by many to be the finest, but the robust flavor of the large buds can work magic in spicy dishes.

CRAB CAKES WITH FRIED GREEN TOMATOES, CORN CREAM, AND SMITHFIELD HAM

4 servings

Ingredients for the Crab Cakes

2 whole eggs

3 tablespoons water

1 cup breadcrumbs

3/4 cup grated Parmesan cheese

1 teaspoon red pepper flakes

1/4 cup mixed chopped fresh herbs (such as chives, parsley, tarragon)

1/2 white onion, finely diced

2 cloves garlic, finely chopped

1 pound jumbo lump crab meat, strained and picked of the shells

12 oyster crackers, crushed (more may be needed for desired consistency)

zest of 1/2 lemon

dash of Tabasco sauce

1/2 red pepper, finely diced

1/2 bunch chives, finely chopped

2 tablespoons chopped parsley

mayonnaise, just enough to bind

salt and pepper to taste

vegetable oil, for frying

Ingredients for the Corn Cream

4 ears of corn, kernels cut from the cob

1 1/2 cups heavy cream

dash of Tabasco sauce

1 teaspoon sugar

salt and pepper to taste

Method for the Crab Cakes

- In a bowl, combine the eggs and water to form an egg wash and set aside. In another bowl, combine the breadcrumbs, Parmesan cheese, pepper flakes, and herbs and set aside.

- Sauté the onion and garlic in a little bit of vegetable oil for about 1 minute and let cool. Combine the rest of the ingredients with the onion and garlic. Divide the mixture evenly and form into 4 cakes.

- Dip the cakes into the egg wash, then coat with the breadcrumb mixture. Fry the crab cakes in a little bit of oil until golden brown.

Method for the Corn Cream

- Heat 1/2 of the corn kernels with the cream in a saucepan. Season with the Tabasco sauce, sugar, salt, and pepper. Bring to a boil and cook for about 1 to 3 minutes, or just enough to cook the corn. Meanwhile, cook the other 1/2 of the corn in enough water to cover (seasoned with salt, pepper, and a pinch of sugar).

- Purée the creamed corn in a blender or food processor for 2 to 3 minutes, or until very smooth. Remove to another pot. Strain the corn kernels cooked in water and add them to the puréed mixture. Mix well and adjust the seasoning. Keep warm.

recipe continued on page 44

Ingredients for the Caper Aioli

1 1/2 cups mayonnaise

juice and zest of 1 lemon

2 tablespoons chopped fresh herbs
(such as chives, parsley, tarragon)

2 tablespoons chopped capers

salt and pepper to taste

Ingredients for the Mustard Tarragon Vinaigrette

2 teaspoons Dijon mustard

1/2 teaspoon chopped shallots

1 tablespoon tarragon vinegar

1 tablespoon red wine vinegar

2 tablespoons chopped fresh tarragon

salt and pepper to taste

4 tablespoons extra-virgin olive oil

1 tablespoon peanut oil

Ingredients for the Tomato and Ham Salad and the Fried Green Tomatoes

2 medium tomatoes, cut into 1-inch cubes

1/2 cup Smithfield ham, cut into very fine julienne

2 scallions, cut into 1-inch pieces,
then sliced julienne

1/2 small red onion, cut into very fine julienne

1/4 cup cornstarch

1/2 cup all-purpose flour

salt and pepper to taste

2 medium green tomatoes,
sliced into rounds about 1/3 inch thick

vegetable oil, for frying

Method for the Caper Aioli

- Combine all the ingredients and adjust the seasoning.

Method for the Mustard Tarragon Vinaigrette

- Combine all the ingredients except the olive oil and peanut oil and allow to sit for about 10 to 15 minutes. Slowly whisk in the oils until well combined. Reserve.

Method for the Tomato and Ham Salad and the Fried Green Tomatoes

- Combine the first 4 ingredients and toss with the mustard tarragon vinaigrette.

- Combine the cornstarch and flour and season with salt and pepper. Dredge the green tomatoes in the flour mixture and fry in the vegetable oil until golden brown.

- Spoon equal amounts of the corn cream on 4 salad plates. Divide the salad among the plates and top with the crab cakes and fried green tomatoes. Drizzle the caper aioli around the rims of the plates and serve.

POTATO-CRUSTED ROCKFISH WITH BUTTERED CABBAGE, MUSTARD CREAM, AND SHERRIED BEETS

4 servings

Ingredients for the Fish

2 Idaho potatoes

1 teaspoon lemon juice

1 tablespoon clarified butter

salt and pepper to taste

4 6-ounce rockfish fillets

vegetable oil, for frying

Ingredients for the Mustard Cream

1/2 cup crème fraîche

1/4 cup Dijon mustard

1/4 cup whole-grain mustard

Ingredients for the Cabbage and the Beets

1 large cabbage head, cut into 1 1/2-inch squares

2 tablespoons butter

salt and pepper to taste

3 to 4 large beets

2 tablespoons sherry vinegar

2 tablespoons walnut oil

Ingredients for the Red Onions and the Swiss Chard

2 red onions, sliced julienne

1 tablespoon walnut oil

salt and pepper to taste

2 heads Swiss chard

2 tablespoons butter

Method for the Fish

• Peel the potatoes and grate on a box grater. Immediately toss with the lemon juice to help avoid oxidation. Hand-squeeze to dry as much as possible, toss with the clarified butter, and season with salt and pepper.

• Cover each fish fillet with some of the grated potatoes to form a crust when cooked. Heat a sauté pan over medium heat. When hot, add a little vegetable oil and carefully lay the fish, potato side down, in the pan and cook until golden brown. Then turn and cook the other side. If the fish is not cooked through, it can be finished in a 350°F oven until done.

Method for the Mustard Cream

• Combine all the ingredients and keep cold.

Method for the Cabbage and the Beets

• Cook the cabbage with the butter until wilted and sweet but still holding in a bit of water. Season with salt and pepper and set aside.

• Roast the beets in a 375°F oven until cooked through and tender, about 1 hour. Set aside until cool enough to handle.

• Peel the beets and dice into 1/4-inch pieces. Season with sherry vinegar, walnut oil, salt, and pepper.

Method for the Red Onions and the Swiss Chard

• Toss the onions in the walnut oil and season with salt and pepper. Place on a cookie sheet and roast in a 350°F oven until tender and golden brown. At the last minute, wilt the Swiss chard in a bit of water and the butter, and season with salt and pepper.

• To serve, spoon a serving each of the cabbage, the beets, the red onions, and the Swiss chard on the bottom of each plate. Place a piece of fish on top of the vegetable medley and drizzle the entrée with the mustard cream.

1789 CHERRY PIE

8 servings

Ingredients for the Dough

3 cups all-purpose flour

3/4 teaspoon salt

1 1/2 teaspoons sugar

9 tablespoons cold butter,
cut into 1/2-inch cubes

4 tablespoons half-and-half

Ingredients for the Filling

1 1/2 pounds pitted sour cherries, fresh or frozen

3/4 cup sugar

2 tablespoons lemon juice

1/4 cup cornstarch

2 1/2 tablespoons cold water

Method for the Dough

- Combine the dry ingredients. Incorporate the cubes of cold butter quickly with the tips of your fingers until the flour is slightly granular and pea-size lumps have formed. Add the half-and-half and mix until combined. Allow to rest in the refrigerator for at least 1 hour.

Method for the Filling

- If the cherries are fresh, cook 1/2 of them just until they are soft and the juice is released. Drain and reserve the juice and put the cherries aside.

- If the cherries are frozen, thaw, then drain and reserve the juice and put the cherries aside.

- Bring about 1 cup of the cherry juice and the sugar to a boil.

- Mix together the lemon juice, cornstarch, and water until smooth. Add this mixture to the boiling juice, stirring constantly until the juice comes back to a boil and the consistency is thick. Remove from the heat, strain, and stir in the reserved cherries. Allow to cool before using.

Method for Assembling the Pie

- Roll out 1/2 of the dough into at least a 10 x 10-inch rectangle about 1/8 inch thick. Cut the rectangle into 1-inch strips. Draw a circle the size of the outer edge of the pie pan on a piece of parchment paper. Place the parchment on a cookie sheet. Arrange the strips in a lattice pattern on the parchment using the drawn circle as a guide. Place in the freezer until ready to use.

- Roll out the remaining dough into a 12-inch circle about 1/8 inch thick.

- Line the bottom of the pie pan with the rolled-out dough. Fill with the cherry filling. Remove the lattice from the freezer and flip over onto the pie. Trim the edges, if needed, to allow for crimping in a decorative pattern. Crimp the edges and bake in a 375°F oven for about 45 minutes, or until the filling is bubbling and the crust is golden.

A SEASON FOR SHAD

In the Philadelphia area, springtime officially arrives when the shad start running in the Delaware River. Lambertville, New Jersey, opens the season with its annual shad festival, and those who love to fish and to eat shad are euphoric for the short time these fish come back to spawn in the rivers where they were born.

The American shad is the largest member of the herring family, and these silvery, torpedo-shaped fish spend most of their time in the salt water along the Atlantic and Pacific coasts. Like salmon, they are anadromous, meaning they can survive in fresh or salt water, preferring the former for laying their eggs. As early as December, the shad start to appear in the rivers of northern Florida. As waters warm with spring weather, they make their way northward into the rivers of the Mid-Atlantic and finally up to New England, ending their journey in June.

Their wide range and the rapid delivery of air freight shipments make fresh shad available for almost half the year, but in each local spawning area the shad run for only a few weeks. Because they feed heavily before they make their runs upriver, "shad season" is the only time the fish are good to eat. During the rest of the year, when they remain in salt water, they tend to be dry and scrawny.

The Pilgrims learned about American shad from the Indians, who taught them not only how to prepare the fish for cooking but also how to bury them among cornstalks for fertilizer. At that time, shad were so plentiful that during their season the new settlers were startled to see the silvery fish nearly choke certain waterways. Shad was a favorite of George Washington, whose troops were given rations of dried shad, and of Thomas Jefferson, who attempted to stock his Monticello pond with the fish. Its popularity grew, and by the mid-1800s over 50 million pounds of shad had been caught on the East Coast.

In the late 1800s, the Eastern shad population was in decline due to river damming, pollution, and overfishing. In 1871, the newly formed United States Fish Commission transported recently hatched American shad to the Sacramento River, introducing the species to the West Coast. Shad thrived in their new home, but Western diners preferred to eat only the shad roe. When shad became scarce in the East, Western shad were shipped in to meet the demand.

In 1965, a five-year, $25 million anadromous fish program was initiated by Congress to protect shad and other fish that swim upriver to spawn, and it was this conservation effort that was responsible for shad's great comeback on the East Coast. Once again, the shad sparkling in Eastern rivers heralds springtime as an American native finds its way home.

Shadtime

The Winnepesaukee Indians were well known for inviting neighboring tribes to their annual shad celebrations, and early American settlers elevated "shadtime" to holiday status. Both Indians and settlers probably implemented the planked cooking style common in Native American cookery. Yet the group that got all the credit for cooking the first planked shad was an esoteric club that held its meetings on the banks of the Delaware River.

The Schuylkill Fishing Company, as it was called, listed Generals Washington and Lafayette among its members and proclaimed itself the first angling and gourmet club in North America. Thirteen times a year, members sporting straw hats and aprons convened in a one-room wooden building to cook their most recent catch. During shadtime they nailed the fish to white oak planks that were propped at 70-degree angles next to the cooking fire. The grilled shad was served at an enormous teak table and greeted with toasts of Madeira all around.

Shad Roe

Female shad are more highly valued than their male counterparts, not only due to their size and flavor but also because they contain the delicious shad roe. Since shad have a defined spawning period, the roe is usually uniform in size, and ideally should resemble small birdshot. It is normally sold in "sets" at fish markets, where it has already been prepared for cooking. If the roe is removed from freshly caught shad, it should be washed and the outer membrane removed. Shad roe takes only minutes to cook and can be simmered just until firm or briefly baked or broiled. It is excellent on its own or chopped and added to other recipes.

SHAD ESCABECHE

4 servings

Ingredients

1/3 cup olive oil

4 small, skinless, and boneless shad fillets (about 2 pounds of fish)

salt and pepper to taste

1 onion, thinly sliced

1 green bell pepper, sliced

1 red bell pepper, sliced

1 tablespoon garlic, finely chopped

1 carrot, peeled and coarsely grated

1 cup tomatoes, diced

1 cup white wine vinegar

1 cup dry white wine

1/2 teaspoon saffron

2 scallions, chopped

zest of 1/2 orange

zest of 1 lemon and 1 lime

2 bay leaves

3 sprigs thyme

1/4 teaspoon crushed red pepper flakes

1/2 cup fresh basil, chopped

slices of lemons and limes

Method

- Heat the olive oil in a sauté pan. Season the fish with salt and pepper and quickly pan-sear it on both sides (it does not have to be cooked all the way through). Transfer the fish to a bowl.

- Add the onion to the sauté pan and cook briefly, without browning. Add the bell peppers and garlic and cook over high heat, stirring, for about 5 minutes.

- Add all the remaining ingredients except the basil and the citrus slices and adjust the seasonings if necessary. Cook over high heat for about 10 minutes, stirring occasionally.

- Pour the mixture over the fish fillets and allow to cool.

- Cover the bowl with plastic wrap and refrigerate for at least 8 and up to 24 hours. Serve cold, garnished with the chopped fresh basil and the lemon and lime slices.

CHEF'S TIP:

Shad are notoriously bony, but don't let that deter you from enjoying this wonderful fish. Buy your shad from a reputable fishmonger and ask to have it filleted before you bring it home.

SHAD SALAD

4 servings

Ingredients

3/4 pound small red bliss potatoes,
scrubbed and cut into quarters

1 1/2 pounds poached shad fillets, skin and
pin bones removed (smoked shad also works
well in this recipe)

1 small red onion, sliced

1 small carrot, peeled and coarsely grated

1 celery stalk, finely diced

3 tablespoons fresh tarragon, chopped

1 red pepper, thinly sliced

2 ears of corn, steamed, kernels cut from the cob

1/4 cup olive oil

1/4 cup lime juice

salt and pepper to taste

red oak lettuce, for garnish

Method

- Boil the potatoes in their skins for about 15 minutes, or until just tender. Cool by running cold water over the potatoes, and drain.

- In a bowl, combine the potatoes with all the remaining ingredients except the red oak, being careful not to flake the fish too much. Line 4 plates with the red oak leaves and top with the fish salad.

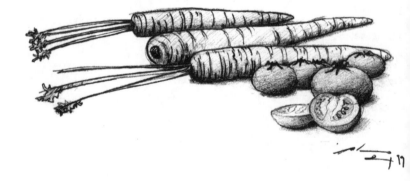

FRIED SHAD FILLETS À LA MEUNIÈRE

4 servings

Ingredients

2 tablespoons olive oil

1 tablespoon plus 2 more tablespoons European-style butter (such as Keller's)

3/4 cup all-purpose flour

1 teaspoon garlic powder

1/2 teaspoon onion powder

1/2 teaspoon fresh thyme

1/2 teaspoon fresh oregano

1/2 teaspoon paprika

1/2 teaspoon ground cumin

1/8 teaspoon cayenne (optional)

salt and pepper to taste

2 pounds shad fillets, skin and pin bones removed

3 teaspoons lemon juice

sauce of choice (optional)

4 lemon wedges

2 tablespoons chopped fresh parsley, for garnish

Method

· Heat the olive oil and 1 tablespoon of the butter in a large sauté pan. In a bowl, mix the flour with the garlic powder, onion powder, thyme, oregano, paprika, cumin, cayenne, salt, and pepper. Coat the shad with the flour mixture and shake off the excess.

· When the fat is hot but before the butter has browned, put the fish in to fry. Turn the fish over when it begins to appear opaque and crisp on the edges, and continue to cook just until it is opaque all the way through. This will take from 2 to 10 minutes, depending on the thickness of the fish. Remove the fish and drain on paper towels. Arrange on a serving plate.

· Discard the remaining butter and oil in the pan. Clean the pan with paper towels and put it back on the heat. Melt the remaining 2 tablespoons of butter in the pan. When it bubbles, add the lemon juice. Swirl the sauce around the pan and pour some over each piece of fish. Serve with lemon wedges, and garnish with the chopped parsley.

CHEF'S TIP:

In French, *meunière* means "miller's wife," someone sure to always have flour on hand in the kitchen. The term refers to food that has been lightly dusted in flour and simply cooked in butter.

ALL-AMERICAN FOURTH OF JULY

On the Fourth of July, Americans wave flags and march to celebrate life, liberty, and the pursuit of happiness. Parades are integral to this holiday, and so is food. Between the festivities and the dazzling fireworks, barbecues sizzle across the land in a smoky symphony. These backyard feasts are reminiscent of the first time citizens gathered together to revel in their independence.

The first official Fourth of July was celebrated in 1777 in Philadelphia, the city where the Declaration of Independence had been signed exactly one year earlier. The streets were laced with banners, and candles glowed in every window. Thirteen-gun salutes boomed from ships in the harbor, and heaping platters of food lined tables all over town. Because barbecued meats were already a common part of colonial celebrations, they were served in abundance as the city rejoiced in the new holiday.

Spanish explorers first learned about barbecued foods from Native Americans, and in a combination of Spanish and Indian dialects the term *barbacoa* was born. The first colonists adopted the technique of cooking meats over a grated fire, and by the early 1600s barbecue feasts featuring whole roasted sturgeons and hogs were fashionable in the Virginia settlements. These happy, social gatherings became traditional up and down the East Coast, and the popular concept rolled westward with the pioneers.

The 1777 jubilee in Philadelphia was the first of many political celebrations perfumed with barbecue smoke. A hundred years later, political speeches and patriotic bands had become as important to barbecues as the meat itself. The large outdoor get-togethers were the perfect forum for stumping candidates. According to *Harper's Weekly* in 1896, votes were won by men who "holler right, vote straight and eat as much barbecue as any other man in the county."

The heated political debates at these events seem mild compared to the fiercely staked claims for the country's finest barbecue. The style and taste of barbecue evolved differently in each region, producing a range of flavors, techniques, preferred meats, and even equipment. Widespread bragging gave way to official contests, in which competitors still guard their recipes and procedures as though they were government secrets.

Despite their differences, those who grill outdoors agree that the barbecue tradition is very much a part of this country's culinary heritage. On the Fourth of July, from Texas to the Carolinas, Kansas City to the streets of Philadelphia, lids clanging on backyard grills ring as true as the Liberty Bell, proclaiming our inalienable right to plate up this all-American bill of fare.

MORSEL

Molasses

Molasses, a by-product of the sugar refining process, was first imported to the American colonies from the West Indies as an ingredient for rum. Because it was cheaper than sugar and more plentiful than honey or maple syrup, it found its way onto American kitchen tables, where it reigned for years as the country's best-selling sweetener. It was so popular that England created the Molasses Act, which placed the same kind of high tariffs on molasses as had been imposed on the colonists' tea. The tariff was widely boycotted, prompting John Adams to call molasses "an essential ingredient in American independence."

MORSEL

Ice Cream

A Fourth of July celebration would be incomplete without scooping up some cold and refreshing ice cream. Although forms of this tasty treat have been enjoyed for thousands of years in other parts of the world, in this country we think of ice cream as being as American as apple pie. An American coined the term "ice cream" in Annapolis, Maryland, in 1744, and by 1777, the confection was regularly being sold in New York, Baltimore, and Philadelphia.

A few years later, simple ice cream–making machines became available to the public; George Washington was one of the first Americans to own one. Thomas Jefferson, with the help of his favorite hostess, Dolley Madison, further boosted the patriotic appeal of ice cream by frequently serving it to guests at the White House.

Lobster Ravioli in Tomato Basil Broth, page 136

Vegetable Soup with Veal Meatballs in Le Bus Sesame Semolina, pages 9-10

Potato-Crusted Rockfish with Buttered Cabbage, Mustard Cream, and Sherried Beets, page 45

Herbed Loin of Lamb with a Goat Cheese and Olive Sauce, page 96

Clams in Apple Cider, page 89

Spicy Buttermilk Fried Chicken, page 128

Beef Stew, page 5

INDEPENDENCE DAY BARBECUED RIBS

4 to 6 servings

Ingredients

6 pounds loin back ribs or spareribs

Melting Pot Marinade (recipe follows)

Backyard Barbecue Sauce (recipe on page 56)

Method

- Place the ribs in a non-reactive container. Pour the Melting Pot Marinade over the ribs, turning to coat. Cover and refrigerate the ribs overnight.

- Prepare the grill. Grill the ribs over low heat, turning occasionally, for 1 1/2 hours, or until done. During the last 30 minutes of cooking, brush the ribs several times with Backyard Barbecue Sauce. Remove the ribs from the grill and cut them into serving pieces.

MELTING POT MARINADE

Ingredients

2/3 cup soy sauce

1/4 cup olive oil

6 cloves minced fresh garlic

2 tablespoons chopped lemon grass

2 tablespoons grated fresh ginger

2 teaspoons Dijon mustard

2 tablespoons molasses

2 tablespoons chopped shallots

Method

- Combine all the ingredients and pour over selected meat.

BACKYARD BARBECUE SAUCE

Ingredients

1 cup ketchup

1 tablespoon Worcestershire sauce

2 or 3 dashes bottled hot pepper sauce

1/2 cup soy sauce

1/4 cup cider vinegar

3 tablespoons brown sugar

2 tablespoons grated fresh ginger

1/2 bunch scallions, chopped

1 tablespoon Dijon mustard

3 tablespoons diced white onion

Method

- Combine all the ingredients in a saucepan over medium heat. Bring to a simmer and cook for 30 minutes.

BACON, LETTUCE, AND TOMATO SALAD

4 servings

Ingredients

4 or 5 pieces of French bread

2 tablespoons olive oil

2 cloves garlic, halved

1/2 head romaine lettuce, rinsed and dried

1/2 head red or green leaf lettuce, rinsed and dried

1/2 head frisée, rinsed and dried

1/2 cup Shallot Vinaigrette (recipe on page 57)

3 ripe tomatoes, cut into 8 wedges each

8 slices bacon, crisply cooked and coarsely crumbled

1 cup crumbled blue cheese

Method

- Brush the bread with the olive oil and rub with the cut side of the garlic cloves. Cut the bread into 1/2-inch cubes. Toast the cubes in a warm (225°F) oven until dry, about 2 hours.

- Line a salad bowl with romaine leaves. Toss together the leaf lettuce and frisée with the Shallot Vinaigrette and put in the center of the bowl. Arrange the tomatoes, bacon, and blue cheese on top of the greens.

SHALLOT VINAIGRETTE

Ingredients

2 tablespoons champagne vinegar

1 teaspoon chopped fresh garlic

1 tablespoon chopped shallots

1 teaspoon Dijon mustard

salt and pepper to taste

1/3 cup olive oil

Method

- Combine all the ingredients except the olive oil in a small bowl. Allow the mixture to stand for at least 15 minutes to blend the flavors. In a steady stream, whisk the olive oil into the vinegar mixture until completely incorporated.

ROASTED CORN COLESLAW

4 servings

Ingredients

2 ears of fresh or thawed frozen corn, kernels cut from the cob

4 cups thinly sliced red cabbage

1/2 cup finely chopped onion

1/4 cup julienne-sliced green bell pepper

1/4 cup julienne-sliced red bell pepper

salt and pepper to taste

1/2 to 3/4 cup mayonnaise

2 tablespoons cider vinegar

Method

- Roast the corn kernels in a 375°F oven for 10 minutes. Allow to cool.

- Combine the corn, cabbage, onion, and bell peppers and chill thoroughly. Just before serving, add salt, pepper, mayonnaise, and vinegar and toss lightly.

LIBERTY BELL HOT BANANA SHORTCAKE

4 servings

This dessert is designed to be made outdoors, as part of a barbecue picnic.

Ingredients

1/4 cup European-style butter (such as Keller's)

2 or 3 green-tipped bananas, peeled and quartered

2 tablespoons lemon juice

2/3 cup brown sugar

1/4 teaspoon cinnamon

4   1-inch slices of pound cake

vanilla ice cream or sour cream

Method

- Melt the butter in a foilware pan over hot coals. Add the bananas, drizzle with lemon juice, and sprinkle with the brown sugar and cinnamon. Cook until the bananas are just soft, spooning the syrup over them occasionally. Meanwhile, toast the slices of pound cake on both sides on the grill.

- To serve, place the warm cake slices on plates and spoon bananas and syrup on top. Top with scoops of ice cream or dollops of sour cream.

WINING AND DINING

One of the first things Leif Erikson noticed as he and his men clambered from their boats onto North American soil was vines, thick with fat, purple grapes, stretching as far as he could see. The abundance prompted him to name the place "Vinland the Good," and he sailed home to report his discovery of this remarkably fertile country.

Early European settlers were equally impressed, and they immediately set out to make wine. Despite their high hopes, these first American vintners were disappointed with the final product. Although the wild vines were rich with fruit, the wine was decidedly different from the wines of Europe. Wine from the fruitier, coarser-tasting American grapes, *Vitis labrusca,* was labeled "foxy" by the colonists, who were used to the more subtle flavors of the European *Vitis vinifera.*

The colonists reasoned that European vines would thrive on American soil just as the native grapes did, and they embarked on a long series of unsuccessful experiments to cultivate imported vines. The land so nurturing to the hardy American species was too harsh for the tender roots of the plants' European cousins (which later adapted perfectly on the West Coast). The European vines were also highly susceptible to a root-eating parasite that did not affect the native American grape plants.

The colonists were persistent, however, and by crossing different strains of American vines and grafting Old World varieties onto New World stock, they began to produce wines agreeable to the European palate. The country's first commercial winery was the Philadelphia Vine Company, which pressed its product along the banks of the Susquehanna River beginning in 1793. The industry gained momentum, and in the nineteenth century spread into the Midwest and northward into what would become the most important wine-making area in the East: the Finger Lake and Hudson Valley regions of New York.

Like other cultures all over the world, Americans not only drank their native wine, they also used it in their cooking. Beginning with the ancient Greeks and Romans, people realized that wine cooked into food stimulates the appetite and acts as a digestive aid. Cooks learned that the glycerin in wine helps to bind sauces, and its intense flavor allows for a reduction of salt in recipes.

American cookery, influenced by waves of immigrants, incorporates wine in a variety of creative ways. California is the most productive wine region in the country, but vintners from coast to coast have matured to produce a very interesting array of native wines.

MORSEL

Riesling Wine

One of the world's best-loved wine grapes is the Riesling, a native of Germany. In vine-yards nestled near the Rhine, Riesling grapes have been cultivated for at least two thousand years. The rest of the world developed an appreciation for the delicate grape, and Riesling wines are now barreled in all the wine regions of Europe as well as in Australia, South Africa, California, and New York. Rieslings are white wines characterized by a spicy, fruity flavor that can range from dry to very sweet. They make wonderful additions to seafood recipes and are often a good choice to serve with a fish dinner.

Rosé Wine

The name rosé comes from the French word for "pink" and refers to the delicate color of this family of wines made from red grapes. Unlike the fermentation process for red wine, in the process for rosé wine the grape skins are removed after two or three days, which leaves the wine with its soft color but without the robust characteristics of red wines. These light-bodied wines are usually somewhat sweet and pair nicely with desserts. In this country, rosé is often referred to as blush wine, white zinfandel, or cabernet blanc.

MORSEL

Rivendell Vineyards and Winery

The peaceful setting that was so favored by the painters of the Hudson Valley School is also home to some of the most picturesque and productive vineyards in the United States. Nestled at the edge of the Catskill Mountains and only a little more than an hour away from the hubbub of New York City, the Rivendell Vineyards and Winery is representative of the best the Eastern wine industry has to offer.

Proprietor Bob Ransom believes in Old World pride and craftsmanship but uses state-of-the-art equipment to produce the most award-winning wines in the Hudson Valley. His dramatic, modern facilities and beautiful grounds were featured on the "Wining and Dining" segment of Flavors of America.

STEAMED MUSSELS WITH WINE AND HERBS

4 servings

Ingredients

2 cloves garlic, minced

2 shallots, minced

1/2 cup Riesling wine

2 tablespoons European-style butter
(such as Keller's)

2 plum tomatoes, diced

2 scallions, chopped

1/2 teaspoon fresh thyme, chopped

1/2 teaspoon fresh basil, chopped

juice of 1/2 lemon

1 bay leaf

salt and pepper to taste

24 mussels, scrubbed, beards removed

Method

- Bring all the ingredients except the mussels to a boil in a large saucepan. Add the mussels and reduce the heat until the mixture just simmers. Cover and cook for about 5 minutes, or until the mussels open. Discard any unopened mussels.

- Place the mussels and the liquid in a large bowl. Serve with a fresh loaf of French bread.

BRAISED VEAL OSSO BUCO WITH RED WINE AND PORTOBELLO MUSHROOMS

4 servings

Ingredients

4 12- to 14-ounce veal shanks
(each 1 1/2 inches thick)

salt and pepper to taste

1 cup (more or less) all-purpose flour

1/2 cup clarified European-style butter
(such as Keller's)

24 small pearl onions, peeled

1 tablespoon chopped garlic

1 celery stalk, cut into 1-inch diagonal slices

1 pound portobello mushrooms, stems removed,
cut into 1/2-inch x 3-inch slices

2 carrots, peeled and cut into 3/4-inch dice

1 14-ounce can crushed tomatoes, with juice

3 cups red wine

1 quart beef stock

5 sprigs fresh parsley

3 tablespoons chopped fresh parsley

1 teaspoon dried thyme

1 teaspoon dried sage

1 teaspoon dried oregano

2 bay leaves

Method

• Season the shanks with salt and pepper and dredge them in some of the flour, shaking off the excess. Heat the butter in a large, deep frying pan or saucepan over moderate heat. Add the shanks and brown on all sides, about 10 minutes. Remove the shanks and place them on a platter.

• Add the onions, garlic, celery, mushrooms, and carrots to the frying pan and sauté for about 5 minutes. Add the tomatoes and cook for 5 more minutes. Sprinkle in about 2 tablespoons of the flour and combine it with the vegetables.

• Deglaze the pan with the wine. Put the veal back in the pan and add the beef stock and herbs. Cover and cook for about 2 hours, adding more stock if necessary. The osso buco is done when the meat falls from the bone. Ladle the meat and vegetables into soup bowls and serve.

MARINATED STRAWBERRY ROSE PARFAIT

4 servings

Ingredients

6 cups strawberries, halved

1 cup rosé wine

8 egg yolks

8 tablespoons sugar

2 cups crushed chocolate cookies

Method

• Marinate the strawberries in the wine for 1 hour. Strain the berries, reserving the liquid, and purée them in a food processor or blender.

• In the top half of a double boiler, mix the egg yolks and sugar with a whisk until well blended. Slowly stir the reserved wine into the egg mixture, whisking continuously, until the mixture coats a spoon, about 5 to 8 minutes. Remove from the heat and let the custard cool completely in the refrigerator.

• Spoon 1 tablespoon of the crushed cookies into each of 4 parfait glasses. Top with a small amount of puréed strawberries, then with custard. Repeat alternating layers, ending with the custard. Sprinkle with the rest of the cookie crumbs. Cover with plastic wrap and refrigerate until ready to use.

VICTOR ORSINI AND VINCE NIGRO

— *Zuppa*: Italian Soups —

Like that of many other chefs, the inspiration for Victor Orsini and Vince Nigro's cooking comes from childhood memories. Their savory Italian specialties are derived from recipes handed down through generations, and their approach to delicious food and culinary style is steeped in the tradition of family kitchens.

Orsini credits his mother, Wanda, with being his culinary muse. She grew up in the mountains of northern Italy, nurtured by the rich culinary heritage of the area. After she immigrated to Philadelphia, she prepared the memorable foods of her homeland in her American kitchen. The flavors and aromas "hypnotized" her son, brought his senses to life, and drew him into the kitchen—a room he never left.

In Vince Nigro's house, Sunday dinner was a major event. Every child participated in the making of the meal and was responsible for specific tasks. Even though they are now grown, Nigro and his siblings still make the trip to their mother Ann Nigro's house on Sundays, food in hand.

These important family traditions formed the basis of both men's love and understanding of good food. Both went on to study under influential chefs and worked in hotels and fine restaurants in the Mid-Atlantic area. In 1993, they teamed up to work for the Rykoff/Sexton Company, a leading full-line distributor with a reputation for quality food products.

Orsini and Nigro represent the company by traveling around the country and giving cooking seminars at sales meetings, using the products the company produces. Their colorful personalities and unique style of cooking flavor their informative and entertaining demonstrations, emphasizing that time spent in the kitchen should be fun. With pure, high-quality ingredients and a technique that is simple and "a bit raw," the men share in their cooking what Orsini calls "a metaphor for how we should live our lives."

MORSEL

Parmesan Cheese

There are many imposters, but true Parmesan cheese is called Parmigiano-Reggiano and comes only from a small area in northern Italy. The cheese originated hundreds of years ago in Bibbiano, a rural town in the Reggio Emilia district adjoining Parma, where most of the cheese trade during the Middle Ages took place. Through the years, the making of this specific grana (granular) cheese was limited to an area that encompassed Parma, Reggio Emilia, Modena, and parts of Bologna and Mantua. It is a commodity so valued by the region that in 1954 the Italian government decreed that the area had sole rights to using the cheese's official name, and it issued laws governing its production.

Parmigiano-Reggiano is painstakingly produced under the strictest standards. The milk used to make the cheese comes from particular herds of cattle that have grazed in specific pastures. The cheese is made only from mid-April to mid-November to ensure that the cattle feed upon fresh grass during production time. The cheese is formed into wheels that must weigh between 66 and 88 pounds, and it must age at least two years before it goes to market. In 1964, the cheesemakers' union began stamping the name Parmigiano-Reggiano on the rind of these special cheeses to prove to consumers that what they were buying was indeed the real thing.

PAPPA AL POMADORO

6 servings

This bread and tomato soup is a celebrated Tuscan preparation.

Ingredients

1/2 cup olive oil

1/2 medium onion, chopped

2 tablespoons chopped fresh garlic

8 cups chicken stock

8 cups peeled, seeded, and cooked plum tomatoes

2 large loaves of Italian bread, trimmed of crust and cut into cubes

1/2 cup chopped fresh basil

salt and pepper to taste

Romano and Parmesan cheeses, for garnish

1 teaspoon Pesto (recipe on page 68), for garnish

Method

• Heat the olive oil in a large stockpot over medium heat. Add the onion and cook until tender. Add the garlic and cook for 1 more minute. As the garlic begins to brown, add the chicken stock and tomatoes and bring the mixture to a simmer. Add the bread and the basil. Continually stir the soup until the bread cubes are mashed and very soft. Season with salt and pepper. Serve hot or warm and garnish with a sprinkle of Romano and Parmesan cheeses and the Pesto.

MINESTRONE

6 servings

Ingredients

1/2 cup olive oil

2 ounces pancetta or bacon, finely diced

1 cup diced onion

1 cup diced celery

1 cup diced carrot

2 zucchini, quartered and sliced

2 leeks, trimmed white parts only,
thoroughly rinsed and cut into 1/4-inch slices

2 cups plum tomatoes, peeled and seeded

8 cups chicken stock

1/2 cup chopped fresh basil

1 pinch thyme

1 pinch marjoram

1 bay leaf

1 cup ditalini pasta, uncooked

1 cup soaked, uncooked kidney beans

2 cups escarole

salt and pepper to taste

Romano and Parmesan cheeses, for garnish

1 teaspoon Pesto (recipe on page 68), for garnish

Method

- Place the olive oil and pancetta or bacon in a stockpot on medium heat. To it add the onion, celery, and carrot. Cook until the onion is translucent. Add the zucchini, leeks, tomatoes, and chicken stock. Bring to a simmer. Add the basil, thyme, marjoram, and bay leaf. Continue to simmer for approximately 20 minutes. Add the pasta, beans, and escarole. Season with salt and pepper to taste. Serve hot or warm and garnish each serving with Romano and Parmesan cheeses and the Pesto.

PESTO

3 cups

Ingredients

4 1/2 ounces pine nuts

1 cup grated Romano cheese

4 cups basil leaves

1 teaspoon black pepper

1 1/2 cups extra-virgin olive oil

Method

- Finely grate the nuts in a food processor. Add the cheese, basil, and pepper and process until finely minced. Slowly add the olive oil while the processor is running. Process the pesto until it is smooth.

STRACCIATELLA

6 servings

In Italian, the name of this soup means "torn rags," which is what the eggs resemble after they are poured into the soup.

Ingredients

8 cups chicken stock

salt and pepper to taste

pinch of nutmeg

2/3 cup pastina, stelline,
or acini di pepe, uncooked

2 eggs

1 teaspoon Romano cheese

1 teaspoon Parmesan cheese

Method

- Bring the chicken stock to a simmer and season with salt and pepper. Add the nutmeg. Add the pastina and cook according to package directions. Beat the eggs and cheeses together. Slowly add the egg mixture to the simmering stock. Stir gently and serve.

HERBS IN THE KITCHEN

Not long ago, most recipes called for dried herbs because fresh were rarely available. Now, a wide variety of cultivated herbs are displayed at most markets, and they are all the rage in the kitchen. People who love to cook are rediscovering the potential of these savory plants, which have been flavoring foods and soothing ailments for thousands of years.

Today's herbal renaissance can be attributed to a few new trends. One is a greater emphasis on healthy eating. Salt, butter, and heavy sauces have given way to natural flavor enhancers such as low-fat stocks and herbs. Another is more regional cooking, which took off when chefs around the country tipped their toques to their predecessors by researching authentic old recipes and making the most of local food products. Herbs are at the heart of many historic dishes, and their innovative use in modern regional cooking forms the basis of many signature flavors. Additionally, the influx of world cuisines over the years revealed a whole new universe of herbs to American cooks. As a result, today's food shoppers are as familiar with cilantro and lemon grass as they are with parsley and mint.

Herbs are more popular than ever in home gardens. Most herbs grow as weeds in the wild and require far less than a green thumb to thrive. Many are perennials and with very little care return each year with gusto. Gardeners can experiment with varieties not usually stocked at stores, such as lemon thyme, opal basil, and pineapple sage. Homegrown herbs can be cut and dried at the end of the season, or potted and brought inside to winter on a windowsill. A convenient way to stock recipe-ready fresh herbs throughout the year is to purée them with a bit of water, stock, or oil, then freeze in ice cube trays.

Most herbs are very pungent and should be added with a light touch in order to do their subtle work in recipes. Dried herbs have a stronger flavor than fresh, and they should be used in smaller quantities. Beyond that rule of thumb, cooking with herbs offers endless possibilities. There are no real taboos about which herbs to use with certain foods. Today's chefs love to experiment with them, trying different flavor combinations in unexpected ways.

MORSEL

Rosemary

Rosemary's ability to endure all kinds of weather is probably why it became symbolic of both life and death in ancient times. Greek and Roman bridal bouquets contained rosemary as a sign of fertility, and at funerals rosemary sprigs were tucked into the hands of the dead. In the Middle Ages, it was viewed as a curative for treating baldness, liver ailments, infections, and the jitters. For good measure, rosemary was also said to repel moths and evil spirits. With all of its attributes, it is a wonder that the heady, pungent flavor of rosemary ever made it to the dinner table. While it may not live up to all of its historical hype, rosemary is certain to work wonders in your recipes.

Lemon Verbena

Unlike most herbs, which arrived in this hemisphere courtesy of European settlers, lemon verbena got its start in the South American area now known as Chile and Peru, where it grows into trees as tall as 10 feet. Impressed by its powers to soothe upset stomachs, Spanish explorers took it back to Europe; there, herbalists also found it effective against depression and headaches. In the kitchen, lemon verbena offers all the flavor of lemon zest without any of the bitter taste. It also makes a refreshing addition to liqueurs and pot potpourri, and has been used in the art of perfume making.

Sage

Sage was appreciated on our continent long before we craved it in our Thanksgiving stuffing, but it is not indigenous to the Western Hemisphere. It is a Mediterranean native that set sail with Spanish explorers and found favor with the Native American tribes of the Southwest. Like the Celtic druids and ancient Chinese herbalists, tribes such as the Navajo believed sage had spiritual and medicinal powers. Elders burned the herb in sweat-bath ceremonies to drive away unfriendly feelings. To this day, some Native Americans wave small, burning bundles of sage in a room to purify the air.

Mint

One of the many quaint customs in Elizabethan England was to plant garden paths with mint. Not only was it attractive, it also perfumed the air when bruised by strollers' feet. Mint was strewn over the floors of banquet halls for its aroma and also to repel the fleas of dogs that sat under the table. Of course, we learned to enjoy its flavor as well, and mint is now the most widely used herb in printed recipes. The mint family is host to over two thousand species, but only spearmint and peppermint carry any commercial weight in the United States. More exotic varieties, such as pineapple, orange, apple, and even chocolate mints, can be found in season at some farm stands and nurseries.

SPLIT PEA AND BULGUR WHEAT SALAD WITH ROSEMARY

4 to 6 servings

Ingredients

1 cup bulgur wheat

1/2 cup green split peas

1/2 cup yellow split peas

2 cloves garlic, finely chopped

1 quart chicken stock

2 medium tomatoes, seeded
and coarsely chopped

1 tablespoon finely chopped fresh rosemary

1/2 tablespoon chopped fresh mint

1 tablespoon chopped fresh parsley

juice of 1 lemon

juice of 2 limes

salt and freshly ground black pepper to taste

1 large red onion, finely chopped

1 celery stalk, finely chopped

1 large carrot, scraped and finely chopped

2 teaspoons olive oil

toasted pita chips

Method

• Place the bulgur wheat in a bowl and pour in enough boiling water to cover it by 1 inch. Let the wheat soak for 30 minutes, then strain in a colander. Press to remove the excess water.

• In a large soup pot, combine the green and yellow split peas. Add the garlic and chicken stock, then cover and bring to a boil. Reduce the heat to a simmer and cook for 30 to 40 minutes, or until the peas are tender.

• In a small bowl, blend together the tomatoes, herbs, lemon and lime juices, salt, and pepper. In a large bowl, combine the split peas and the bulgur wheat. Add the onion, celery, and carrot. Whisk the olive oil into the herb and lemon mixture and pour the dressing over the salad. Toss well. Serve with toasted pita chips.

Note: It is best to let the salad sit for an hour before serving to allow the flavors to meld.

CHEF'S TIP:

For a fancy presentation, spoon the salad into metal rings (available at specialty kitchen stores) and unmold upon plates lined with salad greens.

HERBED ROASTED CHICKEN BREAST WITH CITRUS BUTTER AND MUSHROOM RAGOUT

4 servings

Ingredients

3 tablespoons European-style butter
(such as Keller's), softened to room temperature

1 tablespoon mixed citrus zest
(lemon, lime, or orange)

4 8- to 10-ounce chicken breast halves

1/2 teaspoon chopped fresh tarragon

1/2 teaspoon chopped fresh thyme

1/2 teaspoon chopped fresh sage

1/2 teaspoon chopped fresh oregano

salt and pepper to taste

1/4 cup dry white wine

3 large shallots, cut into thick slices

2 cloves garlic, finely chopped

8 ounces fresh button mushrooms, thinly sliced

Method

• Preheat the oven to 450°F.

• Thoroughly combine the butter with the citrus zest. Form the butter into a log and roll it up in plastic wrap or parchment paper. Place it in the refrigerator to chill.

• Place the chicken breasts on a rack in a roasting pan. Rub the herbs over the chicken to cover the skin and chicken meat. Roast the chicken for 15 to 20 minutes, or until done. Transfer the chicken to a platter and top each breast with 1/4 of the citrus butter.

• Place the roasting pan over high heat and deglaze it with the white wine, scraping up any browned bits at the bottom of the pan. Pour this liquid into a saucepan. Add the shallots and garlic and cook for 1 minute. Add the mushrooms and cook until the liquid has almost evaporated, about 7 to 10 minutes.

• Divide the mushroom mixture among 4 plates and top with the chicken breasts.

CHEF'S TIP:
The same herb mixture used here is a natural for your Thanksgiving turkey; just increase the quantity of the ingredients to accommodate the size of the bird.

LEMON VERBENA AND TARRAGON PANNA COTTA WITH RASPBERRIES

4 servings

Panna cotta is the Italian term for cooked cream. This light custard is usually served cold, with a fruit or chocolate sauce.

Ingredients

16 ounces low-fat lemon yogurt

6 tablespoons sugar

1/4 cup egg whites

2 teaspoons unflavored gelatin powder, softened in 2 tablespoons cold water

1 1/2 teaspoons chopped fresh tarragon

2 teaspoons chopped fresh lemon verbena

1 pint raspberries

Method

• Combine the yogurt and 4 tablespoons of the sugar and mix until thoroughly blended.

• Whip the egg whites until frothy. Slowly add the remaining 2 tablespoons of sugar and continue to whip until the egg whites are stiff.

• In the top half of a double boiler, heat the softened gelatin over simmering water until melted. Remove the pan from the heat and add a small amount of the yogurt mixture to the gelatin. Stir until well blended. Then add the remaining yogurt and stir well. Blend in the tarragon and lemon verbena. Fold in the egg whites to complete the panna cotta mixture.

• Fill 4 8-ounce ramekin molds half full with the panna cotta mixture. Place 5 or 6 raspberries in the middle of each ramekin, and top with the remaining panna cotta mixture.

• Place the ramekins in the refrigerator until they are well chilled and the gelatin has set.

• To unmold, set the ramekins in a bath of hot water for a few moments, then turn the panna cotta onto dessert plates. Serve with additional fresh raspberries and other assorted fruit.

MAGNIFICENT MUSHROOMS

People have been fascinated with mushrooms for centuries. These curious-looking fungi have inspired folklore and religious rites and have provided medical remedies as well as deadly poisons. Mushrooms are not vegetables; they are spore-grown organisms whose appearance and potential danger marked the first mushroom eaters as either very brave or very hungry. They found their way into our diet when we learned what their smoky flavor and meaty texture could do for other foods, and through the years they have become intrinsic to cuisines around the world.

Mushroom cultivation began in Asia thousands of years ago, but it took longer for the idea to catch on in the Western world. Europeans didn't try farming the fungi until the French minister of agriculture under Louis XIV began to experiment with the common white variety we buy most frequently today. By the time Napoleon rose to power, large quantities of mushrooms were carefully being grown in the cool, damp quarry tunnels near Paris.

In America, mushrooms were first cultivated commercially in 1896 near Philadelphia in Kennett Square, Pennsylvania. For over a century, Kennett Square growers have shipped their crops across the country, and today they provide almost 50 percent of the nation's supply, or over 300 million pounds annually. At first, only the common white mushroom was grown in the area. In the past decade, as buyers have become more knowledgeable and the American palate has matured, some Kennett Square farms have concentrated on more exotic varieties such as portobello, oyster, and shiitake. The crops are grown in the dark, inside stone buildings that are climate-controlled to ensure flavor consistency and freshness year-round.

The mushroom industry grosses over $1 billion a year worldwide, using sophisticated growing methods and equipment. We've come a long way since medieval foragers presumed mushrooms magically sprang up where lightning bolts hit the ground, yet mushrooms continue to weave enchantment in our kitchens today.

MORSEL

Shiitake

The white button mushroom may be the world's most common edible fungus, but on Asian tables the shiitake rules supreme. It is indigenous to the Far East, where people learned to farm it over two thousand years ago, making it the world's oldest cultivated mushroom. Shiitakes take their name from the shii, a Japanese tree upon which they sometimes grow. Also known as "perfumed mushrooms," these woody-stemmed, flat fungi have a pungent aroma when cooked and can hold their own in a mixture of flavorful ingredients. As a bonus, they are reputed to reduce cholesterol.

Cremini

These cousins to the white button mushroom look like they have a suntan, but their darker color does not mean they have passed their prime. In fact, cremini mushrooms offer a little more depth in flavor than their snowy counterparts.

Portobello

The broad, flat caps of portobellos can be as large as your hand, and their size and chewy texture make them perfect replacements for meat in a variety of presentations. Commercially sold portobellos are cultivated, but their woodsy flavor allows them to masquerade as wild mushrooms in certain recipes. They are delicious simply brushed with olive oil and thrown on the barbecue to accompany any meal (and unlike the smaller varieties, this jumbo mushroom won't slip through the grill).

Oyster

There is something fishy about oyster mushrooms, even though their name is derived from their color and shape rather than from their flavor. Some people claim that these mushrooms taste faintly of scallops and have even substituted them for the shellfish in recipes. Their delicate taste is marvelous for blending together the flavors of other ingredients.

Duxelles

The classic preparation of duxelles consists of minced mushrooms mixed with herbs and shallots, all sautéed in butter. This versatile concoction, which is used to enrich soups, sauces, and stuffings, is a favorite of chefs, who often add a few choice ingredients of their own. In fact, it was one of the world's most famous chefs who devised the original recipe. Pierre François de la Varenne's claim to fame was writing the definitive book on the emerging French cuisine, Le Cuisinier François, in 1651. He went on to memorialize his employer, the Marquis d'Uxelles, with this savory dish.

SPINACH AND SHIITAKE SOUFFLÉ

4 servings

Ingredients

finely grated Parmesan cheese,
to coat soufflé cups

8 ounces fresh spinach, washed and trimmed

2 tablespoons European-style butter (such as
Keller's) (plus a little more to butter soufflé cups)

1 tablespoon chopped shallots

1 tablespoon minced garlic

7 ounces shiitake mushrooms,
stems removed, sliced

1 cup milk

3 tablespoons all-purpose flour

6 large eggs, separated

salt and pepper to taste

1 tablespoon chopped fresh tarragon

pinch of nutmeg

1 cup finely grated Gruyère or Swiss cheese

Method

- Preheat the oven to 375°F. Butter 4 soufflé cups and sprinkle with the Parmesan cheese.

- Steam the spinach for approximately 1 minute. When it is cool enough to handle, squeeze it to remove excess moisture, then chop it roughly.

- In a medium to large sauté pan over high heat, melt the butter and sauté the shallots and garlic for 1 minute. Add the mushrooms and continue cooking for about 7 minutes, until their liquid is released and has evaporated.

- Purée the mushroom mixture and the spinach in a food processor, then set the purée aside in a large mixing bowl.

- Measure 3 tablespoons of the milk into a small mixing bowl. Whisk in the flour and egg yolks. Bring the remaining milk to a boil in a saucepan over medium-high heat. Slowly stir the boiling milk into the bowl, stirring constantly to avoid cooking the eggs. Return the mixture to the pan and allow it to simmer over low heat until thickened, about 3 minutes.

- Remove the pan from the heat and pour the egg mixture into the bowl with the spinach and mushrooms. Season with the salt, pepper, tarragon, and nutmeg, add the Gruyère or Swiss cheese, and combine thoroughly.

- In another small mixing bowl, beat the egg whites until they form medium-soft peaks. Fold them into the spinach mixture.

- Divide the soufflé among the soufflé cups and bake for approximately 20 minutes, or until lightly browned. Serve immediately.

CHEF'S TIP:
Shiitakes and spinach are a natural flavor blend, but any mushroom would work in this recipe. If you substitute dried, reconstituted mushrooms, reduce the amount you use because their flavor is stronger.

CREMINI MUSHROOM CALZONE WITH BABY MIXED GREENS

4 servings

Ingredients

2 tablespoons clarified European-style butter
(such as Keller's)

1 red onion, peeled and sliced

1 pound cremini mushrooms, quartered

1 yellow bell pepper, sliced

salt and pepper to taste

1 tablespoon finely chopped fresh cilantro

1 tablespoon fresh basil, sliced into thin ribbons
(chiffonade)

1 pound frozen bread dough, thawed in the
refrigerator overnight, cut into 4 pieces

1 to 2 chipotle peppers, puréed

4 ounces Monterey Jack cheese, grated

1 large egg

2 tablespoons water

1/8 cup balsamic vinegar

1/3 cup olive oil

1/3 pound mesclun mix or baby salad greens

Method

- Preheat the oven to 375°F.

- Heat the butter in a large sauté pan over medium heat. Add the onion and sauté for 2 minutes. Add the cremini mushrooms and sauté for about 7 minutes. Add the yellow pepper and sauté for another 3 to 5 minutes, or until the liquid in the pan has evaporated. Season with salt and pepper. Remove from the heat and stir in the cilantro and basil. Allow the mixture to cool.

- On a floured board, roll each piece of bread dough into a 6-inch circle. Spread 1/4 of the chipotle purée on each piece. Spoon 1/4 of the mushroom mixture on 1/2 of each circle and on top of that sprinkle the cheese.

- Fold the dough over on each circle to make a half-moon shape. Pinch the edges all the way down to seal the bread. In a small bowl, whisk the egg with the water. Brush the top of each calzone with the egg wash.

- Place the calzones on a cookie sheet and bake for approximately 12 minutes, or until golden brown and completely hot. Remove from the oven and allow to rest for 6 minutes.

- Whisk together the vinegar and olive oil and toss with the salad greens. Divide the greens among 4 plates and serve with the calzones.

CHEF'S TIP:
Chipotle peppers are dried, smoked jalapeños. For a different flavor, substitute one fresh jalapeño, and leave in the seeds if you really like it hot. These calzones make a wonderful lunch entrée.

ROTELLI WITH A RAGOUT OF CURRIED PORTOBELLO AND OYSTER MUSHROOMS

4 to 6 servings

Ingredients

3 tablespoons clarified European-style butter (such as Keller's)

1 tablespoon finely chopped garlic

1 yellow onion, finely chopped

1 pound fresh portobello mushrooms, stems removed, cut into fourths

1/2 pound oyster mushrooms, sliced in half

2 tablespoons curry powder

1 cup heavy cream

1/2 cup half-and-half

1/3 cup Riesling wine

2 tablespoons fresh basil, sliced into thin ribbons (chiffonade)

1/4 cup chopped cashews

1/4 cup golden raisins

salt and white pepper to taste

1 pound rotelli pasta, cooked al dente

Method

- Melt the butter in a large saucepan over medium heat. Add the garlic and onion and sauté for 2 to 3 minutes. Add the mushrooms and curry powder and sauté for 7 to 10 more minutes. Stir in the cream and the half-and-half, then add all the remaining ingredients except the pasta and cook for about 5 minutes.

- Put the pasta in the saucepan and cook until heated through. Adjust the seasonings with salt and pepper. Divide the pasta among 4 to 6 bowls and serve.

SUDHA KOUL

— Author of *Curries Without Worries* —

One of the best books about the foods of India was written and published in Pennington, New Jersey. Sudha Koul sat down at her kitchen table to write an Indian recipe book for her family and friends, highlighting the dishes of her native land. Her simple, direct approach to Indian cooking made her book stand out in a cooking category many home cooks find complicated, and the book appealed not only to her relatives but to over fifty thousand other readers as well.

Koul established her tiny publishing company, Cashmir, Inc., in order to publish *Curries Without Worries* in 1983. She sent a copy to the Book-of-the-Month Club and was thoroughly surprised when it was selected as a monthly alternate; it then went on to be featured by two other book clubs, the Paperback Club and the Homestyle Club. Favorable reviews and personal appearances at bookstores further boosted sales. Cashmir printed the book nine times, and Koul went on to sign a deal with Warner Books that took the book to three additional printings—a record that would impress the most successful cookbook authors.

Koul believes that Americans are really ready for Indian food to be mainstreamed into our culture. Ingredients that used to seem exotic and unattainable are turning up on non-Indian menus and supermarket shelves. As Koul demonstrates, Indian food can be remarkably simple to prepare. And the aromatic, scintillating dishes are as healthy as they are delicious.

MORSEL

Yogurt

Yogurt is a staple of Indian food, cooling the palate amid the spice and fire of the fare. Most Indian households make fresh yogurt each night for use the following day. Store-bought yogurt works just as well in recipes, but the process of making this nutritious food is remarkably simple and satisfying.

To make your own yogurt, bring 3 cups of milk (whole or low-fat) to a boil in a stainless steel saucepan. Stir the milk as it heats to prevent it from burning on the bottom of the pan. Remove the milk from the heat and cool it until it is just warm to the touch.

Spread 1 teaspoon of plain yogurt (store-bought or homemade) on the bottom of a glass or ceramic bowl and add the warm milk. Cover the bowl and set it in a dark, warm place overnight, or for at least 8 hours. When a film of clear liquid rises to the top, refrigerate the yogurt to make it firm. Be careful not to stir or jostle it until it has chilled.

MORSEL

Coriander (or Cilantro)

Two of the world's favorite flavorings are derived from the same plant but have no resemblance in flavor. The delicate leaves of the coriander plant, also known as cilantro, add a fresh, clean taste to foods, while the seeds impart a pungent, earthy quality. When cooks incorporate either one into their recipes, they are opening the doors to all kinds of international possibilities. The complex flavor of Indian curries depends in part upon coriander seeds, which are also a key ingredient in Scandinavian pastry and Middle Eastern couscous. Coriander leaves are essential in Latin American, Vietnamese, and Indian cooking.

Throughout history, the coriander plant has had a variety of uses. It was first cultivated three thousand years ago in Egypt, where the seeds were used as funeral offerings. The ancient Hebrews were probably introduced to it there, and it became one of the bitter herbs used in their Passover ritual. Hippocrates and other Greek healers used coriander leaves as a digestive agent, and Romans preserved meat with the seeds. The Chinese believed eating the plant would lead to immortality, and in France it was made into a liquid that could be enjoyed either as a cordial or as a perfume. The English came to appreciate coriander after it was incorporated as one of the ingredients in gin. The root of this versatile plant is used to this day in Thai cooking, where it is minced and added to salads and relishes.

CHICKEN PALLAO

4 servings

Ingredients

1/2 cup butter or canola oil

1 teaspoon cumin seeds

1 medium red onion, chopped

1/2 tablespoon chopped ginger

1 tablespoon chopped fresh garlic

4 cloves

1 small cinnamon stick

8 crushed cardamom pods

2 bay leaves

8 peppercorns

1 boneless breast of chicken,
cut into bite-size pieces

1 teaspoon turmeric

1 teaspoon ground cumin

1 teaspoon ground coriander

1/2 cup yogurt

2 cups basmati rice, washed and drained

4 cups water

salt to taste

large pinch of saffron, soaked in 1/2 cup boiling
hot water

Method

• Heat the butter or canola oil in a large saucepan. Add the cumin seeds, and when they sizzle, add the onion, ginger, and garlic. Stir-fry for a few minutes until golden. Add the cloves, cinnamon stick, cardamom, bay leaves, and peppercorns. Stir-fry for 1 minute, then add the chicken and stir-fry for a few more minutes. Add the turmeric, cumin, and coriander and stir-fry a little longer.

• Add the yogurt, quickly stir it into the chicken mixture, and cook for about 1 minute. Add the rice, stir-fry for 1 minute, then add the water and salt. Stir, bring to a boil, then cover; reduce the heat to low and cook for 10 minutes. Pour the saffron and the water in which it was soaking over the rice. Cover again and continue to cook on low for 5 more minutes. Serve.

A SIMPLE RAITA

2 1/2 cups

Raitas are yogurt and chopped vegetable salads that are cool counterparts to some of the spicier Indian foods.

Ingredients

2 1/2 cups yogurt

1 English cucumber, finely diced

2 hot green chile peppers, seeded and finely diced

1 teaspoon ground cumin seed

1/4 teaspoon ground white pepper

salt to taste

1/2 cup finely chopped fresh coriander (cilantro)

Method

- Mix together all the ingredients. Serve chilled.

SUPERMARKET DAL

3 cups

Dals are earthy, spicy dishes that can be made from a number of dried pulses such as lentils, mung beans, or peas. They can contain a variety of ingredients, but almost always have tomatoes, onions, and lots of spices.

Ingredients

1 cup lentils

2 large tomatoes, chopped

2 cups chopped fresh spinach

2 carrots, diced

salt to taste

2 teaspoons ground cumin

2 teaspoons ground coriander

1 teaspoon turmeric

1 tablespoon butter or oil

1 teaspoon cumin seed

1 small red onion, finely diced

1 tablespoon chopped fresh garlic

1 tablespoon chopped fresh ginger

1 cup chopped fresh coriander (cilantro)

Method

- Place the lentils, tomatoes, spinach, carrots, salt, ground cumin, ground coriander, and turmeric in a heavy saucepan. Bring the mixture to a boil over high heat. Reduce the heat to medium and cook until the lentils are tender, about 15 to 20 minutes.

- In a separate pan, heat the butter or oil, add the cumin seed, and stir. Add the onion, garlic, and ginger and stir-fry until golden brown. Add the onion mixture to the lentils and bring all to a quick boil. Remove the dal from the heat, sprinkle with fresh coriander, and serve.

INDIAN HALVA

2 cups

This is an Indian version of the traditional Middle Eastern confection. The more common ingredients of ground sesame seeds and honey are replaced here with Cream of Wheat and sugar.

Ingredients

4 tablespoons butter

1 cup Cream of Wheat

1 cup sugar

3 cups water

1/2 cup blanched, slivered almonds

1/2 teaspoon ground cardamom

1/2 cup golden raisins

Method

• Heat the butter in a sauté pan and add the Cream of Wheat. Stir-fry for a few minutes until the wheat begins to darken in color. Add the sugar and stir-fry for a few more minutes, until the wheat acquires a light brown color. Add the water and stir. Add the almonds, cardamom, and raisins. Stir and bring to a boil. Reduce the heat to low, cover, and cook for 5 or more minutes, until solid. Serve hot or cold.

A Traditional Chesapeake Crab Bake, page 27

Pork Shumei, page 132

Chicken Pallao, A Simple Raita, Supermarket Dal, and Indian Halva, pages 83-85

Minestrone, page 67

Cremini Mushroom Calzone with Baby Mixed Greens, page 78

Grilled Tenderloin, page 4

Pan-Seared Tuna with Sweet Onion and Black Olive Confit, page 91

JERSEY SEAFOOD

The Jersey shore is famous for the enticing boardwalks and beaches that shoulder the coastline, but the suntanned tourists streaming in and out of the waves might be surprised to learn that the water also harbors one of the largest and most diverse supplies of seafood in the world. Over 175 million pounds of fish and shellfish are harvested along the New Jersey coast every year. The wild catch and the expanding local aquaculture net approximately $100 million annually, making the Garden State, which has long been an agricultural powerhouse, a leader in the fishing industry as well.

Commercial fishing has been prospering in New Jersey for over three hundred years. Early on, European colonists realized the rich potential swimming in the waters of the Mid-Atlantic region. Ships sailing from New Jersey ports hauled in tons of fish and marketed their catch all along the Atlantic seaboard. Today there are over 2,800 commercial seafood harvesters working off the Jersey shore. These professional fishermen utilize the latest technology aboard their fleets and in the ports to ensure a quality product to deliver to consumers.

The sea life along the New Jersey coast is diverse because the location is hospitable to both northern and southern species. Over one hundred different kinds of marketable fish mingle in Jersey waters and are sought after by seafood lovers around the world. High-quality tuna and swordfish are shipped to Japan for the most discriminating of sushi eaters. New Jersey skate and monkfish appear on menus in Paris, and it is estimated that two out of three clams consumed worldwide are harvested in New Jersey.

Top catches include sea bass, flounder, mackerel, lobster, oysters, and crabs. Most of these are brought in at the state's six major seaports, the largest of which is Cape May. The historic town, famed as America's first seaside resort, whose gracious streets are adorned with charming Victorian inns and private homes, is the scene of more pounds of landed seafood than any other port in the Northeast.

The state of New Jersey and its professional fishermen are keenly aware that the area's bountiful waters must continue to provide seafood for future generations. Commercial fleets comply with a broad range of rules and regulations that limit the amount of fish that can be harvested, the size of the nets that can be used, and where boats can fish. These measures, coupled with environmental programs, will ensure a New Jersey catch-of-the-day for years to come.

MORSEL

Jersey Seafood Sampler
The following are a few of the most popular catches off the New Jersey coast.

Black Sea Bass
George Washington must have had a few days off during the Revolution, because he is recorded to have been the first person to hire a boat to fish for black bass off Sandy Hook, New Jersey. Many others have followed suit, making the black sea bass one of the most sought-after fish for sport fishing.

Its high oil content makes this rich and flavorful fish a common sight in Italian and Asian markets and restaurants, where it is often fried or steamed whole.

Cod
New Englanders named a cape in its honor, and the same fish that catapulted the Northeast to the top of the fishing industry winters in New Jersey waters. Cod fishing boosts the bottom line of the state's seafood industry in the coldest months, when the fish appears in abundance on regional menus. Scrod, as it is sometimes called, refers to smaller, younger cod. This is a low-oil fish, making it suitable for all kinds of recipes; it is particularly good in fish chowder.

Monkfish
The monkfish may not win any beauty contests, but its exceptional flavor earned it the nickname "poor man's lobster." All year round, these deep-water fish graze for squid, lobster, and skate off the shore of New Jersey. Originally netted as a by-catch in scallop harvesting, monkfish went unappreciated by Americans for years, and most were shipped abroad. The fish found its way onto trendy American menus in the 1980s, after French nouvelle cuisine popularized it under the name lotte.

Tuna
In the spring and summer, tuna migrate to New Jersey waters, making this meaty fish widely available during the outdoor grilling season. Commercial tuna fishing in the Mid-Atlantic region got underway around 1960, and is now giving long-standing Pacific tuna business some healthy competition.

New Jersey fishermen haul in several different species of tuna, including bluefin (highly prized for sushi), yellowfin, skipjack, and albacore (the backbone of the tuna canning industry). Tuna is high in polyunsaturated fats, which play an important role in reducing serum cholesterol and the risk of heart disease.

> **Oysters**
>
> *Found in the brackish waters of New Jersey's bays and estuaries, oysters have been a regional favorite for centuries. They were a mainstay in the diet of the area's Native Americans and helped stave off starvation for the earliest colonists. Oysters were so plentiful that colonial streets in Philadelphia were lined with oyster shells, and even during the Depression oyster dinners (meals consisting only of a variety of oyster dishes) were regular events in the city. In 1847, to complement the area's ample supply of the bivalve, two New Jersey brothers concocted the tiny biscuits that would become universally known as oyster crackers.*

CLAMS IN APPLE CIDER

4 servings

Ingredients

2 tablespoons unsalted European-style butter (such as Keller's)

1 medium onion, thinly sliced

2 large cloves garlic, finely chopped

1/3 cup peeled and finely diced butternut squash

1 small carrot, scraped and cut into thin rounds

salt and pepper to taste

1/4 cup roughly chopped parsley leaves

1 large head curly leaf lettuce, thinly sliced

2 plum tomatoes, diced

1/3 cup fresh apple cider

4 dozen littleneck clams, well scrubbed

Method

• Melt the butter in a large saucepan over high heat. Add the onion, garlic, squash, and carrot. Sauté for 3 to 4 minutes. Season with the salt and pepper. Stir in the parsley, lettuce, and tomatoes. Add the cider and slowly bring to a boil.

• Place the clams in a single layer in the saucepan. Cover, reduce the heat to medium, and simmer until all clams are open, about 5 to 10 minutes. Discard any unopened clams.

• Ladle the clams and broth into soup bowls and serve with a nice loaf of bread.

SALAD OF BEER BATTER–FRIED OYSTERS

4 servings

Ingredients for the Beer Batter–Fried Oysters

1/2 cup all-purpose flour

1/3 cup fine blue cornmeal
(if not available, use yellow)

1 teaspoon baking powder

1 teaspoon paprika

salt and white pepper to taste

3/4 cup beer, at room temperature

1/2 teaspoon olive oil

whites of 3 large eggs

16 oysters, either fresh-shucked or in the juice

Ingredients for the Salad

1/8 cup fresh lemon juice

1 small tomato, diced

1/2 teaspoon dried dill weed

salt and pepper to taste

1/3 cup olive oil

1/3 pound mesclun salad mix or baby greens

Method

- To prepare the beer batter, combine the flour, cornmeal, baking powder, paprika, salt, and pepper in a medium bowl and stir well. Whisk in the beer and olive oil and allow the batter to rest for 45 minutes to 1 hour.

- Whip the egg whites until stiff and fold them into the rested batter.

- Place 1 quart of oil in a 3-quart pot and heat over medium-high heat. Test the oil by dropping a teaspoon of the batter into it to make sure that the batter fries and does not sink.

- Coat the oysters in the batter and fry for 3 to 5 minutes, or until golden brown. Adjust the heat as necessary.

- Combine the lemon juice with the tomato, dill, salt, and pepper. Whisk in the olive oil to make an emulsion, then toss the dressing with the mesclun mix, coating well.

- Place 1/4 of the salad in the center of each of 4 plates and place 4 oysters around the greens.

PAN-SEARED TUNA WITH SWEET ONION AND BLACK OLIVE CONFIT

4 servings

Ingredients

2 large sweet or yellow onions, thinly sliced

2 cups dry white wine

1 tablespoon brown sugar

1 teaspoon dried oregano

salt and freshly ground black pepper to taste

10 calamata olives, pitted and roughly chopped

1 tablespoon clarified European-style butter (such as Keller's)

4 8-ounce tuna steaks

Method

• Put the onions and wine in a medium saucepan over medium-high heat, cover, and cook for about 1 hour, until the onions are tender. Uncover and add the brown sugar, oregano, salt, and pepper and cook until the liquid has almost evaporated. Stir in the olives and remove the confit from the heat.

• Place the butter in a nonstick sauté pan over high heat. Season the tuna steaks with salt and pepper. Add them to the pan and sauté until golden brown on each side, approximately 5 minutes, or until medium-rare to medium on the inside.

• Divide the confit among 4 dinner plates and top each serving with a tuna steak.

GOAT CHEESE, NOW AN AMERICAN DELIGHT

Nearly every American chef cites goat cheese as a favorite ingredient, and its popularity is evident on trendy menus across the country. Not that long ago, however, it was viewed as a highbrow French extravagance with an overly aggressive aroma. For years, the only goat cheese available on this side of the Atlantic was imported, and it was only as fresh as the sixty-day waiting period required by the Food and Drug Administration allowed. Unlike most cheeses, goat cheese is at its best when it is relatively fresh; significant aging impairs its flavor. The longer it sits, the stronger its flavor and aroma become, and the barnyard bouquet and hefty imported price tag kept most Americans at bay.

The transformation of goat cheese from exotic to favored food in the United States is due, in large part, to American dairy farmers who have mastered goat cheese making. Before a few visionary entrepreneurs took the goat by the horns and made its fresh cheese available in this country, the age-old process was practiced only in Europe, the Middle East, and India. There, the method of making goat cheese evolved from simple production in goatskin bags to a painstaking art form that is learned through years of experience.

Although a factory-made product is acceptable, especially in cooking, goat cheese aficionados favor the varieties that are made by hand. Instead of being pressed through industrial extruders, handmade goat cheese is carefully ladled into perforated molds of varying shapes and allowed to drain until the proper consistency is reached. It is then shipped as quickly as possible to market.

The mildly tart flavor of fresh goat cheese gives it a distinctive personality that is quite different from cow's milk cheeses. Its different molecular structure causes the fat molecules to be smaller, and as a result many people find goat's milk products easier to digest than those made from cow's milk. It is also relatively low in cholesterol and is an excellent source of calcium, phosphorous, and vitamins A and B.

MORSEL

Coach Farm

For one thousand French Alpine goats, home is Coach Farm, New York—three hundred prime acres of Hudson River Valley farmland. With the help of their innovative and energetic owners, these floppy-eared mountain climbers produce what many rate as America's finest goat cheese. Coach Farm's proprietors, Miles and Lillian Cahn, got into the business on a whim and have since set about learning and mastering the finest methods of goat cheese production.

The same dedication to quality and business expertise that made the Cahns' first business, Coach Leatherware, such a success is apparent in their new enterprise. The couple traveled to France and learned first-hand from farmers who had been making goat cheese for generations. In New York City, they discovered and hired a woman who had spent much of her life in France making cheese. Her invaluable expertise was passed on to other Coach Farm workers, who are proud to make an American product that rivals or even bests some of the cheeses of France.

Today, between 4,000 and 5,000 pounds of handmade goat cheese from Coach Farm are shipped every week to food purveyors and restaurant chefs eager to receive a fresh, high-quality product. The cheeses, which are made in traditional French shapes but have American names, have won dozens of prizes, including the Outstanding Product Line at the 1993 national Fancy Food Show. With all the effort the Cahns have put into their business, it would seem natural for them to take credit for its success. But they are quick to honor their staff, and say that most of the achievement is due to the goats themselves, all one thousand of whom have been named.

Coach Farm was featured on the "Goat Cheese, Now an American Delight" segment of Flavors of America.

GOAT CHEESE, EGGPLANT, AND ROASTED PEPPER TART

6 to 8 servings

Ingredients for the Tart

1/2 pound frozen puff pastry
(thawed overnight in the refrigerator)

2 tablespoons softened European-style butter
(such as Keller's)

3 bell peppers (1 each red, green, and yellow)

1 Japanese eggplant or 2 small American
eggplants

1/4 cup clarified European-style butter

salt and pepper to taste

2 cups crumbled goat cheese, loosely packed

1/4 cup grated Parmesan cheese

16 fresh basil leaves, for garnish

Ingredients for the Salad

1/8 cup balsamic vinegar

salt and pepper to taste

1/3 cup olive oil

1/4 pound mixed salad greens

Method

- Preheat the oven to 400°F.

- Grease a fluted pan, pie tin, or shallow springform pan. Roll out the puff pastry to the width of the baking pan. Dust the rolling pin with flour and carefully roll the pastry back onto the rolling pin, then unroll it over the pan. Press the dough into place and crimp the edges. Brush the pastry with the softened butter.

- Place the bell peppers over an open flame or under the broiler and completely blacken them on all sides. Put the blackened peppers in a plastic bag, seal it, and allow them to steam for 20 minutes. Remove the peppers from the bag and peel away and discard all black skin. Cut the peppers in half and remove all seeds and veins. Cut into 1/2-inch-thick strips.

- Cut the eggplant crosswise on the bias into 1/2-inch-thick slices. Brush the eggplant lightly with the clarified butter and season with salt and pepper. Roast the eggplant in the oven for 15 minutes, or until done but not mushy.

- Place the crumbled goat cheese on top of the pastry. Top the goat cheese with the eggplant and peppers in a spiral fashion, overlapping each. Sprinkle the Parmesan cheese over the eggplant and peppers.

- Bake the tart for about 12 minutes, or until it is golden brown and the edges are puffy. Garnish with the fresh basil leaves.

- Whisk together the vinegar, salt, and pepper in a bowl. Slowly add the olive oil while whisking. Toss with the greens and any remaining eggplant or peppers and serve on top of the tart.

HERBED LOIN OF LAMB WITH A GOAT CHEESE AND OLIVE SAUCE

4 servings

Ingredients

8 lamb loin chops (each approximately 1 inch thick) or 4 4-bone lamb racks

salt and pepper to taste

2 tablespoons clarified European-style butter (such as Keller's)

2 tablespoons shallots, finely chopped

3/4 cup dry red wine

1/2 teaspoon dried basil

1/2 teaspoon dried thyme

2 tablespoons chopped fresh sage

1/4 cup crumbled goat cheese, loosely packed

1/2 cup calamata olives, pitted and sliced lengthwise

Method

• Preheat the oven to 350°F.

• Season both sides of the lamb chops with salt and pepper. Put the butter in a large sauté pan over high heat. When the pan is hot (smoking), add the lamb and sear for approximately 2 to 3 minutes on each side, until golden brown. Finish in the oven to desired temperature.

• In the same sauté pan, add the shallots and sauté for about 1 minute. Deglaze the pan with the wine, scraping the bottom with a wooden spoon to loosen the browned bits accumulated there. Add the basil, thyme, and sage, increase the heat to high, and reduce the liquid to 1/2 cup.

• Reduce the heat, stir in the goat cheese and olives, and correct the seasoning. Place 2 lamb chops on each of 4 dinner plates and top with some of the goat cheese and olive sauce.

GOAT CHEESE BLINTZES WITH BLUEBERRY SAUCE

4 to 6 servings

Ingredients for the Blintzes

16 ounces (about 2 cups) crumbled goat cheese, loosely packed

16 ounces (about 2 cups) large-curd cottage cheese

3 eggs

1/4 cup plus 2 tablespoons granulated sugar

1 teaspoon vanilla extract

1/2 teaspoon grated lemon peel

12 Crêpes (recipe on page 98)

Ingredients for the Sauce

1 pound frozen blueberries

1/3 cup sugar

2 teaspoons cornstarch

1/2 teaspoon grated lemon peel

powdered sugar and whipped cream (optional)

Method for the Blintzes

- Preheat the oven to 250°F.

- In a large mixing bowl, add the cheeses, eggs, sugar, vanilla, and lemon peel and blend well. Line a baking sheet with foil.

- Divide the cheese mixture among the Crêpes and mound in the center of each one. Fold one side of each crêpe over the filling and press gently. Fold in the two ends and press gently. Fold over the remaining side and press to enclose the filling. Place the blintzes seam side down on the foil-covered sheet.

- Bake the blintzes for about 15 to 20 minutes.

Method for the Sauce

- Combine the berries, sugar, cornstarch, and lemon peel in a large saucepan over medium heat. Allow the berry mixture to reduce over medium heat until the sauce has thickened, stirring often. Pour sauce over the blintzes and top with powdered sugar and whipped cream, if desired.

CRÊPES

Ingredients

1 cup flour

3 eggs

1 cup milk (more may be needed to thin mixture)

2 tablespoons melted European-style butter (such as Keller's)

pinch of salt

clarified European-style butter, for cooking

Method

• Combine all the ingredients except the clarified butter, stirring in enough milk to form the consistency of thin cream. Allow the mixture to stand for 30 minutes.

• In an 8-inch nonstick pan, heat 2 to 3 tablespoons of clarified butter, swirl around, and pour the excess into a bowl. Add a small ladle of batter to the pan and swirl the batter around the pan so the pan is completely covered (too much and the crêpe will be thick, too little and it will have holes). The crêpes need to be as close to 8 inches in diameter as possible.

• Fry each crêpe quickly over medium-high heat until golden brown underneath. Flip the crêpe over and cook for about 1 more minute, or until brown. Remove and keep moist under cloth, foil, or plastic wrap. Repeat with the remaining batter.

NICOLA SHIRLEY

— Jamaican Jerk Hut —

Nicola Shirley's mission is to introduce the wonderful flavors of Jamaican cuisine to as many people as possible. Through her very successful restaurant, Jamaican Jerk Hut, and the line of specialty products she produces, she has gone a long way toward achieving her goal.

Shirley spent the first sixteen years of her life on the beautiful island of Jamaica, absorbing its culture and developing a love for cooking, surrounded by the sights and smells of Caribbean kitchens. After her family moved to Philadelphia, she focused on her interest in cooking, mustered her talents, and entered a culinary contest for student chefs. Winning the competition and being named Student Chef of the Year inspired her to attend Johnson & Wales University, from which she earned a degree with honors in hotel, food, and beverage management.

She spent some time in the hotel industry and also in private catering, where she was noted for creating international peace baskets decoratively filled with food and gift items from various countries. The baskets, which benefited the One Percent for Peace organization, were named Best Gift Idea for 1989.

In 1994, Shirley combined her marketing skills with her culinary expertise to open the Jamaican Jerk Hut, which was subsequently awarded "Best of Philly for Caribbean Cuisine" honors by *Philadelphia Magazine*. Her jerk seasoning and table sauce competed and won against industry leaders at the 1996 Fancy Food Show in Philadelphia and are now available in selected stores. Shirley has also developed a natural juice line, which includes drinks like Ginger Beer and Sorrel and Fruit Punch.

When she is not behind the stove, Shirley is active in professional and charitable groups. She is an executive board member of the international women's culinary organization Les Dames d'Escoffier, and she coordinated and hosted the Philadelphia chapter's highly successful 1998 fundraiser benefiting women entering the culinary profession. Always looking for new ideas and projects, Shirley is currently exploring ways to expand her restaurant concept and broaden her specialty product line.

MORSEL

Callaloo

Musical-sounding callaloo is a generic name for the leaves from a family of edible tubers that includes the taro, dasheen, and cocoyam. It is also the name of a Caribbean soup made from these greens. Callaloo leaves are shaped like elephant ears, and their flavor and texture resemble spinach or chard, vegetables that can be substituted in recipes if callaloo is not available.

The leaves and roots are sometimes marketed together under the name "dasheen." The family of plants, which originated in southeast Asia and India, was brought westward by African slaves, whose ingredients and cooking techniques have been among the most important influences in Caribbean cuisine.

MORSEL

Scotch Bonnet Peppers

In the fiery realm of chile peppers, Scotch bonnets have one of the most incinerating reputations. Like with its more widely known close relative the habanero, a little goes a very long way. Scotch bonnet is the pepper of choice in Jamaica, where cooks say its slightly tropical flavor, hinting of mangoes, oranges, and bananas, is the perfect complement to island fare. When they are ripe, Scotch bonnets are flaming red and deep yellow in color, alluding to the power they wield.

CALLALOO TARTS

1 2 t a r t s

Ingredients

1 18-ounce can callaloo (available at specialty markets), or an equal amount of canned or fresh spinach or chard

1/4 cup finely chopped onion

1/4 cup finely chopped bell pepper (red, yellow, or green)

1/4 cup diced plum tomatoes

1/2 teaspoon minced Scotch bonnet pepper

1 tablespoon minced garlic

1 tablespoon chopped fresh thyme

salt and pepper to taste

3 eggs

1 cup heavy cream

1 dozen medium tartlet shells (pastry shells)

Method

- Preheat the oven to 350°F.

- Drain the callaloo and place it in a mixing bowl. Add the onion, bell pepper, tomatoes, Scotch bonnet pepper, garlic, thyme, salt, and pepper and mix well.

- Put the eggs and cream in a separate bowl and mix well. Add this mixture to the callaloo mixture and combine well.

- Spoon the callaloo filling into the tartlet shells. Place the shells on a cookie sheet and bake for 20 minutes.

JAMAICAN BROWN STEW WITH RED SNAPPER FISH

4 servings

Ingredients

1 teaspoon salt

1 teaspoon black pepper

1 teaspoon garlic powder

1 whole 1 1/2-pound red snapper, scaled, gutted, and fins removed

1 1/2 cups vegetable oil

1 tablespoon olive oil

1/4 cup butter

1/2 cup chopped onion

1/2 cup chopped bell peppers (red, yellow, and green)

1 tablespoon minced garlic

1/2 cup diced plum tomatoes

1/4 cup chopped carrot

1/4 cup peeled, seeded, and chopped chocho (see Chef's Tip)

Scotch bonnet pepper to taste, chopped

1 tablespoon chopped fresh thyme

2 teaspoons chopped pimento

salt and pepper to taste

2 tablespoons soy sauce

1/2 cup tomato paste or ketchup

2 cups fish stock, vegetable stock, or water

"Turn" Cornmeal (recipe on page 103)

Fried Plantains (recipe on page 103)

Method

• Mix 1 teaspoon salt and 1 teaspoon pepper together with the garlic powder. Rub the spice mixture over the entire fish and inside the cavity. Heat the vegetable oil in a large skillet and pan-fry the fish on both sides. Remove the fish from the skillet and place on paper towels to remove the excess oil.

• Also remove the excess oil from the skillet, then heat the olive oil and the butter. Sauté the onion, bell peppers, garlic, tomatoes, carrot, chocho, Scotch bonnet pepper, thyme, and pimento. Season with salt and pepper.

• When the onion is translucent, add the soy sauce, tomato paste, and stock or water. Bring to a boil for 5 minutes. Add the red snapper to the pot and correct the seasoning. Cover the pot and allow to simmer for 5 to 10 minutes, or until the fish is cooked. Remove the fish and serve with "Turn" Cornmeal and Fried Plantains.

CHEF'S TIP:

Chocho, a member of the squash family, has a flavor reminiscent of cucumbers and zucchini. It can be purchased fresh or canned at specialty food markets.

"TURN" CORNMEAL

Ingredients

2 tablespoons olive oil

1/2 each of one yellow, red, and green bell pepper, chopped

2 small tomatoes, diced

1/2 onion, chopped

1/2 cup chopped okra

1 tablespoon chopped garlic

1 tablespoon chopped thyme

1 teaspoon whole allspice, crushed

1/2 teaspoon minced Scotch bonnet pepper

salt and pepper to taste

6 cups vegetable stock

1/3 cup coconut milk

1 pound yellow cornmeal

Method

• In a medium saucepan, sauté in olive oil the bell peppers, tomatoes, onion, okra, garlic, thyme, allspice, and Scotch bonnet pepper. Season with salt and pepper. When the onion is translucent, add 4 cups of the vegetable stock and the coconut milk and bring to a boil.

• In a separate bowl, mix 2 cups of the vegetable stock with the cornmeal. Remove the saucepan from the heat, add the cornmeal mixture to the pot, and stir until smooth. Return the saucepan to the stove over medium heat. Stir, or "turn," the cornmeal for 10 minutes. The mixture should be thick and have the consistency of mashed potatoes. Remove from the heat and serve hot.

FRIED PLANTAINS

4 servings

Ingredients

3 ripe plantains (the skin should be yellow with black marks), peeled

1/2 cup vegetable oil

Method

• Slice the plantains on the bias, about 1/4 inch thick. In a sauté pan, heat the vegetable oil over medium heat. Add the plantain chips to the pan and cook, turning, until golden brown on both sides. Drain on paper towels.

JEWISH-AMERICAN
COMFORT FOOD

Jewish food in America is as diverse as the many Jewish groups that have immigrated to this country. American Jews trace their origins to over a dozen countries in Europe and the Middle East, and each culture has played a part in forming American Jewish cuisine. Flavors and techniques from countries such as Germany, Russia, Italy, Hungary, Holland, and Israel have blended in a rich legacy of foods prepared from the heart.

Many customs in Jewish cooking are derived from religious law, which predisposes each cook to careful consideration of ingredients and preparations. To Jews, food has always been viewed as a gift from God, and as such was used to mark every important occasion. Many recipes are symbolic of historical religious events. In many Jewish kitchens, foods must be kosher, meaning they are chosen and combined according to biblical rules. The word "kosher" comes from the Hebrew word meaning proper or pure. When using certified kosher ingredients, cooks can be assured that their foods have been carefully handled and packaged according to rabbinical standards. Kosher meats come from animals that have been fed organic food and killed in the most humane and hygienic way possible. The attention paid to quality and nutrition in kosher food appeals not only to the Jewish cook but to anyone interested in healthy eating.

Steeped as it is in religious tradition, the real powermongers in Jewish cooking are the generations of mothers who have handed down their prized recipes for what many believe is the ultimate comfort food. "Eat, it will make you feel better" was their motto as they lovingly prepared the soups, breads, and savory meats that formed precious childhood memories for thousands of people. Unlike the French and Italian cuisines that rose to prominence under visionary, professional chefs, American Jewish cooking has always been presided over by somebody's mother.

It is its down-home goodness that has attracted all kinds of diners to Jewish cuisine, and people are drawn to the warmth of the family-oriented meals. When a New York advertisement once proclaimed: "You don't have to be Jewish to like rye bread," it might as well have endorsed *all* Jewish-American food.

MORSEL, BY MYRA CHANIN

My Mother's Secret Formula

Making chicken soup was the best way of making the most of this humble bird for the Friday night Sabbath dinner, the culinary high point of the week. For my mother, as for many women of her generation, making soup was more than just cooking, it was a formula for world domination.

The preparation always involved inventing an excuse to persuade your daughter (me) to take you shopping and then making the soup, an eight-hour process, at your daughter's house. Why did it take an entire day to produce a pot of soup? Because it took eight hours to properly lace soup with guilt and love.

Her initial shopping triumph at the kosher butcher shop was getting extra feet to add body and flavor to her soup. Where did these extra feet come from? From somebody else's chicken, of course.

My mother believed butchers hid the best chicken in the walk-in storage refrigerator in the back room of the store for their favorite customers. Did kosher butchers really keep their best hens in the back? When I quizzed them about it, they looked at me like I was insane. Of course, the best birds were in the refrigerator case in the store! So what was in the back? Slightly flawed birds for customers like my mother, who wanted respect and recognition for the excellence of their knowledge of ingredients even more than they wanted first-class birds. The only words my mother wanted to hear from a butcher were, "These chickens are not for you. For you I have some put away in the back."

Next came a half-hour ride to a greengrocer on the other side of town for vegetables worthy of her. From watching my mother shop, I learned how to tell the difference between exceptional and inferior ingredients. The good dill roots, parsley roots, celery, onions, and carrots were always on the very bottom of some ungainly pile.

My mother's next steps in the soup-making process involved cleaning my house from top to bottom and then reminding me of an old Russian proverb, which states that it only takes a few minutes to turn a hovel into a palace, or in my case, vice versa. Only when I scolded her did she actually start making soup. The final step? Lining up all the members of my family to taste the soup and assure her that it was the best soup they ever ate. Did that satisfy her? Of course not. She checked the culinary file cabinet in her tastebuds and replied that five years ago for my Uncle Abe's birthday party, she'd produced a soup that tasted better than this one!

Myra Chanin, also known as "Mother Wonderful," made a guest appearance on the "Jewish-American Comfort Food" segment of Flavors of America. *She is the author of* Mother Wonderful's Chicken Soup, *published in 1997 by Dell.*

HOME-STYLE CHICKEN SOUP

6 to 8 servings

Ingredients

4 quarts water

1 large frying chicken (3 1/2 to 4 pounds), skin removed, cut into quarters

chicken neck and gizzard

2 medium onions, peeled

2 celery stalks, cut in half

1 bay leaf

2 medium carrots, peeled and diced into 1/2-inch pieces

1/2 pound wide noodles, cooked according to package directions

1 tablespoon dried dill weed

salt and pepper to taste

Method

- Bring the water to a boil in a large stockpot. Add the chicken, chicken neck, and gizzard and reduce the heat to medium-low. Simmer the chicken for 10 to 15 minutes, stirring occasionally.

- While the chicken is cooking, use a ladle to skim off the white foam that floats to the top of the soup. When the foam has been removed, add the onions, celery, and bay leaf. Cover the pot, reduce the heat to low, and allow the soup to simmer gently for about 4 hours. (The longer the better.)

- Remove the chicken from the broth and allow to cool. Strain the onions, celery, and bay leaf out of the broth with a slotted spoon and discard. Add the carrots to the broth and simmer for another 15 minutes. Remove the chicken meat from the bones and pull it into bite-size pieces. Add the meat and the cooked noodles to the broth and heat through.

- Season the soup with the dill, salt, and pepper. Ladle into bowls and serve.

WINE-MARINATED BRISKET

6 to 8 servings

Ingredients for the Marinade

2 cups dry red wine

3 tablespoons soy sauce

1 small onion, peeled and diced

1 celery stalk, thinly sliced

2 cloves garlic, finely minced

1   12-ounce can diced tomatoes, with juice

1 tablespoon dried rosemary

1 tablespoon dried thyme

salt and pepper to taste

Ingredients for the Brisket

1   3- to 3 1/2-pound beef brisket,
trimmed of all visible fat

8 new potatoes, peeled and cut into 1-inch cubes

3 carrots, cut into 1-inch pieces

1 medium onion, peeled and thinly sliced

3 celery stalks, cut into 1-inch pieces

Method

• Mix together all the marinade ingredients in a non-reactive baking dish large enough to hold the brisket. Add the meat and marinate overnight in the refrigerator.

• Preheat the oven to 325°F.

• Transfer the brisket to a roasting pan and pour the marinade over the brisket. Cover the pan tightly with foil and roast the brisket, basting occasionally, for 2 1/2 to 3 hours, or until very tender. During the last hour of cooking, add the potatoes, carrots, onion, and celery.

• Remove the brisket and vegetables from the pan to a serving platter. Pour the liquid from the pan through a strainer, skim off the fat, and serve the liquid as a sauce.

OLD-FASHIONED KUGEL

6 to 8 servings

Ingredients

1 pound dried angel hair pasta,
broken into 2-inch lengths

1/2 cup vegetable oil

1/4 cup granulated sugar

1 teaspoon salt

1/2 teaspoon black pepper

4 large eggs, beaten

1/2 cup raisins

Method

- Cook the pasta according to package directions and drain. Set aside.

- Preheat the oven to 325°F.

- Put the vegetable oil and sugar in a 6-quart pot over medium heat. Cook, stirring, for 4 or 5 minutes, or until the sugar melts and turns dark brown.

- Immediately add the well-drained pasta, stirring constantly so that the oil and caramelized sugar are evenly distributed. If the sugar solidifies into chunks, continue stirring the pasta over medium-high heat until the sugar melts.

- Remove the pasta from the pan and stir in the salt and pepper. Let the mixture cool for about 30 minutes, or until lukewarm.

- Stir the beaten eggs completely into the pasta. Fold in the raisins. Place the mixture in an 8- or 9-inch round pan and place it in the oven. Bake for 20 to 35 minutes, or until the top is golden and crisp.

- Allow the kugel to cool for 5 minutes. Slice into wedges and serve.

INSPIRED PASTA

Most Americans cannot resist a plate of steaming pasta. Our appreciation for it dates from colonial times, when English settlers served up their old-country macaroni and cheese dishes. Thomas Jefferson enjoyed pasta dinners abroad so much that he imported the first spaghetti machine to Monticello and proudly served the exotic dish to visiting statesmen. Italian immigrants, lured to the States during the Gold Rush, brought their imported pasta with them. It was not until the shortages of World War I cut off Italian pasta shipments that commercial pasta production in America began in earnest.

Though most people think of pasta as being an Italian food, numerous cuisines offer their own interpretations of pasta dishes. It is easy to understand how this simple, versatile food evolved in some form in almost every ancient culture, although no one knows its exact origin. One widely held myth is that Marco Polo brought the recipe for pasta from China to Italy after his journeys to the Far East in the thirteenth century. In fact, the existence of lasagna, macaroni, and ravioli was documented in Italy long before the famous explorer brought his souvenirs home.

Marco Polo did sample rice noodles in China and would have been interested to know that Koreans claim to have invented the food and were responsible for introducing it to Japan. Solid evidence also exists that India and parts of the Middle East had some form of pasta centuries before Marco Polo's excursions. Perhaps the earliest evidence of pasta was found in the Tuscany region of Italy, where decorations in Etruscan tombs dating from 600 B.C. include scenes of pasta preparation.

Whether or not Italy was the birthplace of this wonderful food, there is little doubt that when it comes to pasta made with wheat, Italians have set the standard and provided the most inspiration. Modern American chefs have created an eclectic array of pasta dishes by borrowing from regional cuisines and ethnic ingredients, but they still take their cue from the techniques and principles that have long guided Italian pasta making. This traditional approach to preparing innovative pasta dishes, combined with deliciously familiar Italian recipes, has inspired Americans to boil up almost 4 billion pounds a year—topping even Italy in pasta consumption.

MORSEL

Dried vs. Fresh Pasta

In the 1980s, commercially prepared fresh pasta began to surface in food markets, and pasta lovers were led to believe it was superior to the factory-made dried variety. Most pasta experts agree that both dried and fresh pasta, though very different from one another, have a role to play in the kitchen.

Egg-based pasta is better when made fresh, and homemade is far superior to the product found in the refrigerated section of grocery stores. Egg-based pasta dough is rolled or stretched to a desired thickness and cut into a variety of shapes. Ravioli is one example of pasta that should always be freshly made with egg dough; the light touch of the hand is appreciated in its tender preparation.

Extruded pasta, such as spaghetti, rigatoni, or macaroni, is simply made from semolina wheat and water. The lack of eggs gives the dough a different consistency, and factories are far better equipped to make and carefully dry these pastas than are home kitchens. The quality of wheat used in the process usually gives imported dried pasta a flavor superior to that of domestic brands.

PASTA AND BEAN SOUP (PASTA E FAGIOLI)

4 servings

Ingredients

1 ounce prosciutto, diced

1 large yellow onion, chopped

2 cloves garlic, finely chopped

1/4 cup olive oil

4 cups chicken stock

1   14 1/2-ounce can diced tomatoes, with juice

1/2 pound small macaroni

1 teaspoon dried basil

1 teaspoon dried marjoram

2   19-ounce cans cannelloni or great northern beans, drained

1/4 cup Parmesan cheese

salt and freshly ground pepper to taste

Method

• In a medium-size soup pot, sauté the prosciutto, onion, and garlic in the olive oil for 2 to 3 minutes. Add the chicken stock and tomatoes with their juice, and bring to a boil.

• Add the macaroni, basil, and marjoram and reduce to a simmer. Cook until the pasta is al dente, stirring constantly. Add the beans, Parmesan cheese, salt, and pepper and serve.

(Remember, the pasta will absorb a lot of the liquid. The soup should be dense, but if it needs additional liquid at the end of cooking, add more stock and warm through.)

ARTICHOKE ASIAGO AND SUN-DRIED TOMATO RAVIOLI

8 servings

Ingredients

1 9-ounce package frozen artichoke hearts

1/2 cup grated Asiago cheese

1/3 cup sun-dried tomatoes preserved in oil, chopped fine

1/4 cup breadcrumbs

3 tablespoons olive oil

1 tablespoon chopped fresh oregano or 1 teaspoon dried oregano

1 tablespoon chopped fresh parsley

2 cloves garlic, finely chopped

1/2 teaspoon grated lemon zest, finely chopped

salt and black pepper to taste

Egg Pasta Dough (recipe follows)

1 egg yolk, for sealing the ravioli edges

2 cups fresh tomato sauce

Method

- Blanch the artichoke hearts in boiling water for 3 minutes, then drain and cool. Squeeze out most of the water by hand, finely chop the artichokes, and place them in a bowl.

- Add the cheese, sun-dried tomatoes, breadcrumbs, olive oil, oregano, parsley, garlic, lemon zest, salt, and pepper. Mix until well combined.

- Roll out the pasta dough as thin as possible, less than 1/16 inch thick. Using a 2- or 3-inch cutter, stamp out 24 circles. Save the unused portion of the pasta dough.

- Drop a heaping 1/2 teaspoon of filling into the center of each round and moisten the edges with some of the egg yolk. Fold the circles over to make half-moon shapes. Firmly press the edges to seal the dough, forcing out any air. Dust the ravioli with flour or cornmeal if not using right away.

- Heat the tomato sauce in a pan and keep warm. In a large pot of boiling water, cook the ravioli until just done, about 6 to 8 minutes. Drain the ravioli and toss with the tomato sauce.

EGG PASTA DOUGH

Ingredients

1 1/2 cups all-purpose flour

3 eggs, lightly beaten

1 tablespoon vegetable oil

1/2 teaspoon salt

Method

- Place the flour on a board and make a well in the center. Add the eggs, vegetable oil, and salt. With your fingers, gradually mix in the flour, adding more flour if the dough is too moist.

- Knead the dough until it is elastic and can form a ball. Cover and allow to rest for 30 minutes to 1 hour.

- Divide the dough into 2 or 3 pieces. Roll, cut, and cook as directed above.

PAN-SEARED RIGATONI WITH SAUSAGE, PEPPERS, AND RICOTTA

4 servings

Ingredients

1 tablespoon clarified European-style butter (such as Keller's)

3/4 pound Italian hot sausage, removed from the casing and crumbled

3/4 pound dried rigatoni, cooked according to package directions

2 red bell peppers, thinly sliced

1 small onion, finely chopped

2 cloves fresh garlic, finely chopped

1/3 cup dry red wine

1 3/4 cups canned crushed tomatoes, with juice

1 cup ricotta cheese

1 teaspoon dried marjoram

1 teaspoon dried basil

salt and freshly ground pepper to taste

2 tablespoons chopped fresh parsley

Method

• Place the butter in a large sauté pan over medium-high heat and cook the sausage until done and brown, about 3 to 4 minutes. Remove the sausage with a slotted spoon and throw away all but 2 tablespoons of the fat in the pan.

• Add the cooked rigatoni to the pan and pan-sear it until crispy and light brown, about 10 to 12 minutes. Midway through cooking the pasta, add the bell peppers, onion, and garlic.

• Deglaze the pan with the wine. Add the sausage, tomatoes, ricotta, marjoram, basil, salt, and pepper. Cook the mixture, stirring occasionally, over medium-high heat for 10 minutes. Divide among 4 plates, sprinkle with the parsley, and serve.

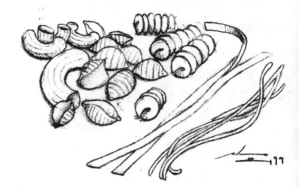

SUSANNA GOIHMAN

— Azafran —

Susanna Goihman was born in Caracas, Venezuela, where her earliest memories were formed in the kitchen of her grandmother, who added "love and spices" to the dishes she prepared for the family. She learned technique and the importance of presentation at the knee of this accomplished cook, who was caramelizing onions and reducing stock before Goihman knew the terms existed. Goihman is a self-taught chef who cites her grandmother's early influence, and in that tradition she tries to impart the warmth and sharing of family dining in her food.

When Goihman was a young child, her family relocated to Miami, where Latin cultures from South and Central America blended with those from the Caribbean and Puerto Rico to offer an exciting arena of music, art, and most importantly, food. Goihman earned a degree in fashion at the Philadelphia College of Textiles, but her love for cooking led her into the catering business in 1994. Inspired by her early experiences in Venezuela and Miami, she began to create eclectic South American cuisine for her delighted customers. In 1997, she opened Azafran in Philadelphia, where she combines the excitement of Latin flavors with American flair, reflecting the heritage she treasures and loves to share.

MORSEL

Plantains

Plantains have always been prominent in African and Indian cooking, and Arab traders brought them from those countries to Europe. Thinking he would introduce the food to the newly discovered Caribbean Islands, a Spanish missionary brought some plantain shoots to plant there. It was later discovered that plantains had been consumed in Central and South America long before the missionary's plants took root in the New World.

Although slightly larger than a banana, the long, waxy plantain is an obvious relative to the more common fruit. While bananas are very sweet, plantains are rather bland and starchy, making them much more versatile in the main courses and desserts of South American cuisine. Their subdued flavor makes them perfect partners for spicy sauces, and their hearty consistency enables them to withstand cooking techniques that range from deep-frying to simmering in stews. Aside from their culinary attributes, plantains are a solid source of carbohydrates, dietary fiber, potassium, carotene, and vitamin C.

SHRIMP AND PLANTAIN ROLLS WITH GINGERED TERIYAKI VINAIGRETTE

4 servings

Ingredients for the Rolls

1 red bell pepper

4 whole shrimp, peeled and deveined

1 very ripe plantain (almost black),
cut into 1-inch chunks

4 egg roll wrappers

1 egg yolk, beaten

oil, for frying

Ingredients for the Vinaigrette

1/4 cup soy sauce

1/4 cup sake or sherry

1/4 cup rice wine vinegar

1 teaspoon sugar

2 teaspoons minced fresh ginger

1 tablespoon vegetable oil

1 clove garlic, chopped

1/8 teaspoon white pepper

Method for the Rolls

- To roast the bell pepper, place it over an open flame, under the broiler, or on the grill. Blacken the skin all over without burning the flesh. Transfer to a bowl, cover with plastic wrap, and allow to steam for about 15 to 20 minutes. Peel away the skin, then remove the seeds and membranes inside. Cut the roasted pepper into pieces the same size as the shrimp.

- Combine the shrimp, plantain, and roasted pepper. Place 1/4 of the mixture on one of the egg roll wrappers and begin to roll. About halfway into rolling, fold the ends in and continue to roll, forming an enclosed log. Brush the inside end of the log with the beaten egg yolk and seal the roll. Repeat this process for the remaining rolls.

- Heat the oil in a frying pan or wok until very hot. Fry the rolls on both sides until golden brown, about 5 to 8 minutes.

Method for the Vinaigrette

- Combine all the ingredients and serve with the rolls.

SUGAR CANE–MARINATED BABY SALMON FILLETS SERVED OVER FRIED RIPE SWEET PLANTAINS

4 servings

Ingredients

1 can sugar cane

1 tablespoon chopped fresh ginger

1 tablespoon chopped fresh garlic

1 bay leaf

1 jalapeño pepper, seeded and cut into rings

1/4 cup rice wine vinegar

1/4 cup olive oil

1/4 cup red wine

4 4-ounce salmon fillets

1 cup vegetable oil, for frying

1 ripe plantain, peeled and thinly sliced lengthwise

Method

· Combine all the ingredients except the salmon, vegetable oil, and plantain. Add the salmon and allow to marinate for 2 hours.

· Heat the vegetable oil in a frying pan over medium heat. Fry the plantain in the oil until golden brown on both sides. Remove and drain on paper towels.

· Remove the salmon fillets from the marinade and pan-sear them until golden brown on both sides. (If the salmon is not done to taste after searing, it can be finished to taste in a 375°F oven.) Divide the fried plantain strips among 4 dinner plates and place the salmon fillets on top.

Herbed Roasted Chicken Breast with Citrus Butter and Mushroom Ragout, page 72

Old-Fashioned Kugel, page 109

Pumpkin Crème Brûlée, page 148

1789 Cherry Pie, page 46

Lemon Verbena and Tarragon Panna Cotta with Raspberries, page 73

Grilled Fruit with Mango Cream, page 152

Goat Cheese Blintzes with Blueberry Sauce, page 97

CILANTRO-MARINATED TUNA STEAKS SERVED OVER FUFU WITH BALSAMIC TERIYAKI GLAZE

4 servings

Ingredients for the Marinated Tuna Steaks

1 bunch parsley

1 bunch cilantro

2 cloves garlic

1 tablespoon oregano

1/3 cup olive oil

1/3 cup fresh lime juice

salt and pepper to taste

1 large onion, coarsely chopped

4 8-ounce tuna steaks

Ingredients for the Balsamic Teriyaki Glaze

1/4 cup soy sauce

1/4 cup sake or sherry

1 teaspoon sugar

1 teaspoon fresh minced ginger

1 clove garlic, minced

1/4 cup balsamic vinegar

Ingredients for the Fufu

4 medium-ripe plantains,
peeled and cut into chunks

3 tablespoons chimichuri (see above)

4 tablespoons butter

Method for the Marinated Tuna Steaks

• In a food processor, finely chop all the ingredients except the onion and tuna. Remove the mixture from the food processor and add the onion. This mixture is called a *chimichuri.*

• Slather all but 3 tablespoons of the chimichuri on the tuna steaks and pan-sear them in a little oil on both sides, taking care to keep the tuna rare to medium-rare.

Method for the Balsamic Teriyaki Glaze

• Combine all the ingredients in a medium-size saucepan and reduce to a glaze.

Method for the Fufu

• Bring 1 quart of water to a boil in a medium saucepan. Boil the plantains until tender, remove from the water, and drain. Add the chimichuri and butter to the plantains and mash together.

• To serve, pile the fufu in the middle of each of 4 dinner plates and place a tuna steak on top. Drizzle with the balsamic teriyaki glaze. This dish can be garnished with fried green plantains and salsa cruda (uncooked, fresh salsa).

PENNSYLVANIA DUTCH DELIGHTS

The Europeans who accepted William Penn's invitation to settle in Pennsylvania embodied the essence of the American spirit. These were people from Germany, Alsace, Switzerland, and other Rhineland areas who left their homelands to pursue the religious freedom promised by the new country. With their focus on beginning anew and bonded by their principles, these people from different Germanic backgrounds came together to form a unique culture, the Pennsylvania Dutch ("Dutch" is derived from *Deutsch*, the German word for their language).

From the time they tilled their first fields in this country, the Pennsylvania Dutch considered themselves completely American. Unlike many immigrants who went to great lengths to maintain their Old World ties, the Pennsylvania Dutch never looked back. As targets of religious persecution in their homelands, they saw their farms destroyed and they fled to America with only the bare necessities. Very thankful for the new home they found, they set to work making the most of the lush acreage around them. The recipes they brought with them were quickly amended to include the cornucopia of foods they discovered here.

Wasting food was tantamount to sin, and the culinary tradition of the Pennsylvania Dutch is rich with clever ways to make use of every edible morsel. Huge kitchens were the focal points in the stone houses that sprang up in the thirty counties of Pennsylvania Dutch country. Built large enough to accommodate the preparation and consumption of three enormous family meals per day, these productive rooms were also where huge canning, curing, and drying operations took place. The Pennsylvania Dutch employed ingenious methods for saving any food that could not be eaten in season, using preservation techniques perfected to maximize flavor.

Today, descendants of the original Pennsylvania Dutch make up approximately 40 percent of the state's population. Of these, about 8 percent are Amish, the religious sect that perhaps most reflects the essence of those first Pennsylvania Dutch settlers. Their focus on hard work and their diligence in avoiding modern influences sets them apart in today's hurried world.

The simple, hearty food of the Amish and other Pennsylvania Dutch is home cooking at its best. This is not a cuisine honed in restaurants and deciphered from cookbooks. It is the work of generations of women standing over family stoves who have handed down cooking traditions and the sense of pride in the land so carefully nurtured by their families.

Shoofly Pie

One of the most famous dishes from Pennsylvania Dutch country is the enigmatically named shoofly pie. In a culture that specializes in pies, this one stands out in popularity. There are many variations of this pie, which was originally served as a breakfast treat, but they always contain one common ingredient: a healthy portion of molasses.

Some people contend that the confection's name comes from the French choufleur, which means cauliflower and refers to the crumbly pie's resemblance to the vegetable. This may be a plausible explanation, since some of the early Pennsylvania Dutch were natives of Alsace-Lorraine. Others contend that the pie is so delicious that a decoy pie must be prepared and set in an open window to lure flies away from the pies that are meant to be eaten. But the most likely explanation is that "Shoofly" was actually the brand of molasses used in the original recipe.

CUCUMBER AND RED ONION SALAD

4 servings

Ingredients

2 medium cucumbers, peeled, seeded, and thinly sliced

1 large or 2 small red onions, thinly sliced

1 red bell pepper, thinly sliced

1 clove garlic, minced

1 1/2 teaspoons prepared mustard

1 tablespoon sugar

2 tablespoons cider vinegar

3 tablespoons mayonnaise

1 tablespoon chopped parsley

1/2 tablespoon chopped fresh dill

salt and pepper to taste

paprika, for garnish

4 whole, fried parsley leaves, for garnish
(To make, fry in 1 cup vegetable oil heated
to 350°F until crisp, about 1 to 2 minutes.)

Method

- In a large bowl, combine all the ingredients except the paprika and fried parsley. Allow the salad to rest for 1 hour, then serve as is, or combine with Bibb lettuce. Sprinkle with the paprika and garnish with parsley leaves.

CHICKEN POTPIE

4 servings

The Pennsylvania Dutch version of this dish replaces the standard pie crust with wide noodles cooked right into the "pie."

Ingredients

2 quarts chicken broth or water

2 8-ounce chicken breasts, cut into 1 1/2-inch pieces

3 medium potatoes, peeled and cut into 1-inch chunks

1 medium onion, diced

2 carrots, peeled and diced

2 celery stalks, diced

1 tablespoon chopped fresh garlic

pinch of saffron

1/4 cup chopped parsley

1/4 teaspoon chopped fresh thyme

1/4 teaspoon chopped fresh rosemary

Potpie Squares (recipe follows)

salt and pepper to taste

Method

- Bring the chicken broth or water to a boil in a large stockpot and add the chicken. Add the potatoes, onion, carrots, celery, garlic, and saffron and cook for about 15 minutes.

- Add the herbs and the Potpie Squares to the broth and cook for about 20 minutes, or until the dough is tender.

- Season with salt and pepper. Ladle into 4 soup bowls and serve piping hot.

POTPIE SQUARES

Ingredients

1 cup all-purpose flour
(plus extra for dusting the cutting board)

1/4 teaspoon salt

1/4 teaspoon dried thyme

1 teaspoon chopped parsley

1 egg

3 1/2 tablespoons milk

Method

- Combine the flour, salt, thyme, and parsley in a bowl. Add the egg and milk, working them together to form a soft dough. Try not to overwork the dough or it will become tough.

- On a floured surface, roll the dough out to the thickness of a nickel. Cut into 1 x 2-inch rectangles.

APPLE DUMPLINGS

4 servings

Ingredients

1 cup all-purpose flour

1 teaspoon baking powder

1/2 teaspoon salt

3/8 cup shortening

1/4 cup milk

2 Red Delicious apples, peeled, cored, and cut in half

cinnamon and nutmeg, for seasoning

Apple Syrup (recipe follows) or bottled maple syrup

4 tablespoons European-style butter (such as Keller's)

Method

- Preheat the oven to 400°F.

- Sift together the flour, baking powder, and salt. Cut in the shortening just until crumbly. Add the milk and stir just until the flour mixture is moistened.

- On a floured surface, roll out the dough just large enough to cut 4 6-inch squares. Place 1/2 apple on each square and sprinkle with a little cinnamon and nutmeg. Pour about 1 teaspoon of Apple Syrup over the apple and dot with 1 tablespoon butter.

- Pull all four corners of the dough up to meet in the middle, moisten the corners, and pinch them together. Be sure to make a sealed package to help "steam" the apple.

- Bake for about 8 minutes.

- Baste the dumplings with the Apple Syrup and reduce the heat to 300°F. Bake for about 20 minutes or until golden brown, basting often. Serve hot, with cold milk and sugar poured over the top.

APPLE SYRUP

Ingredients

1/2 cup water

1/2 cup apple juice

1 1/2 tablespoons apple jack brandy

3/4 cup light brown sugar

1/4 teaspoon cinnamon

1/4 teaspoon nutmeg

1/4 cup European-style butter (such as Keller's)

Method

- Combine all the ingredients except the butter in a small saucepan. Bring to a boil and cook for about 5 minutes. Remove from the heat and whisk in the butter.

VIRGINIA COOKERY

Jamestown became the birthplace of Virginia cookery when British colonists eagerly combined their native cuisine with the wide variety of foods they discovered in their new land. The pioneers who settled in and around Jamestown were more fortunate than some of their northern neighbors, whose weather and terrain were harsh. By contrast, Virginia was brimming with game and fish, and plenty of fruits and vegetables were available during the generous growing season. When it became evident that their English stores were dwindling and prospects for new shipments were unpredictable, the settlers took advantage of the breadth of the bounty surrounding them.

From Native Americans, early Virginians learned to grow and enjoy corn, pumpkins, squash, and potatoes. In addition to indigenous vegetables, early farmers were delighted to find that their European vegetable seeds produced finer crops than they had in their homeland. English farm animals thrived in their new home, and the subsequent ham, lamb, and chicken dinners were supplemented with wild game such as turkey and venison.

Virginia's proximity to Washington, D.C., made it a haven for politicians, even in post-Revolutionary times. Taverns and inns catered to a sophisticated clientele, and the hospitality for which the state is still known was kindled over the tables where legislation was debated. Visitors from every state as well as dignitaries from abroad left Virginia impressed with the delicious fare and the warmth with which it was served.

The gentility cultivated in Virginia was a result not only of the wealth it acquired through its locally grown foods but also of the financial strength the colony gained through its tobacco production and sales. With their increasing wealth, Virginians became more refined. Their tables were laden with the best their region could offer, combined with the elegant European touches they picked up during trips abroad. The most famous example of the Virginia cosmopolitan was Thomas Jefferson. His patriotic endorsement of native foods is legendary, but he was also instrumental in the introduction of sophisticated European cooking techniques and ingredients to his country. The blending of French cuisine with that of the American South—preparing local foods with imported seasonings—became the basis of the Virginia cooking that still rewards hungry visitors and lifelong residents with every bite.

MORSEL

Smithfield Ham

Perhaps the most famous of Virginian foods is the Smithfield ham, which has been produced in the area since colonial times. Before beef rose to prominence in the American diet, pork was the primary domestic meat. The art of ham curing was an important one, and each region specialized in its own method. Though tasty hams are produced elsewhere, many agree that the hams from Virginia are America's best.

Virginia ham was a product of peanut-fed hogs and the particular curing and smoking process developed in the Tidewater town of Smithfield, Virginia. Hams there were salt-cured for weeks, smoked over specially chosen wood for days, then aged for six to twenty-four months, depending upon the desired flavor (the longer the aging, the stronger the flavor). Queen Victoria and Sarah Bernhardt were two of the more celebrated fans of Smithfield hams.

In 1926, in an effort to maintain the standard of the Smithfield ham, the General Assembly of Virginia passed a statute that set strict standards for the regional specialty. Hams could no longer be labeled Smithfield unless they were from peanut-fed Virginian hogs and were cured in the town that gave them their name. But Smithfield is not the only place in Virginia that processes ham. Similarly cured and very flavorful aged hams are made throughout the state and are sold simply as Virginia ham.

SPICED SHRIMP AND WATERCRESS SALAD WITH VIRGINIA HAM VINAIGRETTE

4 servings

Ingredients for the Shrimp

1 cup vinegar

1/2 cup beer (optional)

1 crushed hot Italian pepper or
a dash of Tabasco sauce

2 celery stalks, chopped

2 tablespoons salt

2 bay leaves

1 clove fresh garlic, crushed

2 1/2 pounds shrimp, peeled and deveined

Ingredients for the Salad

2 tablespoons champagne vinegar

1/2 tablespoon chopped fresh garlic

1/2 tablespoon chopped shallots

3 tablespoons Virginia ham, soaked and minced

1 tablespoon chopped parsley

1/2 teaspoon Dijon mustard

1/3 cup olive oil

salt and black pepper to taste

1/2 pound watercress, stemmed and washed

1/2 pound arugula, stemmed and washed

Method

- In a large saucepan, combine all the ingredients for the shrimp, add enough water to cover, and bring to a boil. Reduce to a simmer and cook for 10 minutes. Remove the shrimp from the water and cool.

- Combine the vinegar, garlic, shallots, ham, parsley, and mustard in a small bowl and let stand for 20 minutes to incorporate the flavor of the meat. Slowly whisk in the olive oil and adjust the seasoning with salt and pepper to taste.

- Toss the greens with the dressing and divide among 4 salad plates. Top each serving with 1/4 of the shrimp.

SPICY BUTTERMILK FRIED CHICKEN

4 servings

Ingredients

2 pounds boneless, skinless chicken breasts

1 cup buttermilk

2 tablespoons hot sauce

3/4 cup all-purpose flour

1/4 cup cornmeal

2 teaspoons salt

1 tablespoon garlic powder

1 tablespoon onion powder

2 teaspoons freshly cracked black pepper

2 tablespoons minced fresh mixed herbs
(parsley, oregano, thyme)

1 quart canola oil, for frying

Method

- Trim the chicken breasts, removing fat and tendons. Cut into 2-inch-wide strips. Mix the buttermilk and hot sauce in a large bowl and marinate the chicken overnight in the refrigerator.

- Combine the flour, cornmeal, seasonings, and herbs in a large self-sealing bag. Add the chicken pieces, a few at a time, to the bag and shake in the seasoned flour.

- Heat the canola oil in a large skillet to 350°F. Fry the chicken uncovered in the canola oil, cooking only as many pieces at one time as will fit in without crowding. Turn the pieces after 2 minutes, and cook until golden brown all over.

APPLESAUCE CAKE

8 servings

Ingredients

2 cups flour

1 1/2 teaspoons baking soda

1/2 teaspoon salt

1 teaspoon cinnamon

1/4 teaspoon nutmeg

1/2 teaspoon cloves

3/4 cup shortening

2 cups sugar

2 eggs, beaten

1 1/2 cups applesauce

1 cup chopped walnuts

1 cup raisins

Method

- Preheat the oven to 350°F.

- Sift together the flour, baking soda, salt, cinnamon, nutmeg, and cloves. Put the shortening and sugar in a mixing bowl and cream until well combined. Add the beaten eggs and combine.

- Alternate adding the flour mixture and the applesauce to the egg mixture a little at a time, beating until smooth after each addition, until they are completely incorporated. Fold in the chopped nuts and raisins.

- Pour the batter into a greased loaf pan or suitable baking pan and bake for 1 hour, or until a cake tester comes out clean when inserted in the middle.

THE DELIGHTS OF DIM SUM

In English, *dim sum* means "heart's delight" or "to touch the heart," and its translation is a clue to the real nature of this delightful tradition. In today's fast-paced world, dim sum offers a retreat into an unhurried atmosphere of friendship and sharing.

Dim sum originated in southern China in the province of Canton, where the subtropical climate and healthy economy produced an easy, amiable culture. For over a thousand years, the practice of serving small tidbits with tea in the midmorning and midafternoon has delighted the hearts of the Cantonese. As the Chinese immigrated to Europe and the United States, the rest of the world became acquainted with this gracious custom.

Dim sum has always been a social event, served in teahouses rather than in conventional restaurants or in homes. Friends and people negotiating business deals gather in large, informal facilities that specialize in hundreds of appetizer-size dishes. Amidst the happy, noisy atmosphere, servers push carts loaded with bamboo baskets cradling different mouthwatering tidbits, and they stop at tables when patrons nod or raise a finger. The servers constantly wind through the maze of tables, tempting diners with freshly cooked, spicy, savory, or sweet morsels. Dim sum is not actually considered a meal, although sampling the many selections can be as satiating as any banquet.

Dim sum can last for hours, and all the while a wide variety of teas are offered and poured at each table. Tea is such a key element in the presentation that in Canton, dim sum is sometimes referred to as *yum char*, or "drink tea meal."

In the relaxed atmosphere of dim sum, no one keeps track of what each table orders. When the patrons finally surrender and are ready to leave, the proprietor simply counts the number of plates at the table and charges a set fee for each one. Diners leave, fortified with the delectable flavors of China, warmed by fragrant teas, and with hearts touched by the good cheer of dim sum.

MORSEL

Chinese Five-Spice

Five-spice is a blend of seasonings that adds a mysterious yet irresistible flavor to Chinese cooking. The aromatic combination consists of approximately equal amounts of star anise, Sichuan peppercorns, fennel, cloves, and cinnamon ground together to produce a brown powder. The best five-spice uses top-quality ingredients, which give off a pungent aroma. Chinese chefs use this seasoning extensively in a variety of ways, such as in the marinade for Peking duck.

MORSEL

Bamboo Shoots

The bamboo shoots used in Chinese cooking are the tender, new growth of certain types of bamboo that belong to the grass family. In Asia, hundreds of different kinds of bamboo shoots are marketed fresh in the spring, and fresh shoots are occasionally sold in Chinese markets in the United States. Usually, only canned bamboo shoots are available here, but these are suitable for almost all recipes.

Most supermarkets carry canned bamboo shoots, which are pale yellow, crunchy, and somewhat sweet. Canned shoots are sold whole or thickly sliced, and should be rinsed and blanched in boiling water before using in recipes. Transfer unused portions to a jar filled with water, refrigerate, and use within a few days.

LOBSTER AND SHRIMP POTSTICKERS

3 dozen potstickers

Ingredients

1/2 pound raw shrimp, chopped or ground

1 teaspoon ground dried shrimp, chopped*

1/4 pound cooked lobster meat, chopped

2 ounces pork, chopped fine or ground

1/4 cup bamboo shoots, chopped*

1/4 teaspoon ginger powder

1/4 teaspoon white pepper

1 tablespoon scallions, chopped

pinch of salt

1/2 teaspoon sesame oil*

1 egg white

1 tablespoon dry sherry

1 tablespoon cornstarch

pinch of Chinese five-spice*

wonton skins, for wrapping*

2 tablespoons peanut oil

1 cup chicken stock

shredded cabbage or Bibb lettuce

Soy Vinaigrette (recipe on page 132)

These items can usually be found in the specialty section of the supermarket, and they are always available at Asian food markets.

Method

- In a mixing bowl, thoroughly combine all the ingredients except the wonton wrappers, peanut oil, chicken stock, cabbage or lettuce, and Soy Vinaigrette. Place about 1 teaspoon of the filling in each wonton wrapper. Brush the edges with water and fold the edges over to form half-moon shapes. Press the edges together firmly.

- Put the peanut oil in a wok or sauté pan over high heat. When the oil is very hot, add the potstickers and fry very quickly on both sides. This will take about 2 minutes.

- Add the stock and simmer for about 7 minutes. Serve with shredded cabbage or Bibb lettuce, dressed with Soy Vinaigrette.

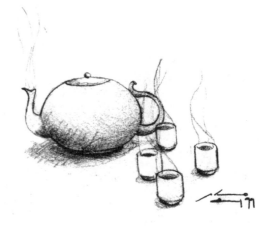

SOY VINAIGRETTE

Ingredients

2 tablespoons balsamic vinegar

1 tablespoon soy sauce

1 teaspoon chopped fresh garlic

1 teaspoon chopped shallots

salt and pepper to taste

5 tablespoons extra-virgin olive oil

Method

· Combine all the ingredients except the olive oil in a small bowl. Pour the oil in a thin stream into the bowl, whisking until it is completely incorporated.

PORK SHUMEI

24 shumei

Ingredients

1 pound ground pork

2 tablespoons dry sherry

2 tablespoons soy sauce

1 teaspoon minced ginger

1/2 teaspoon ground white pepper

1 tablespoon sesame oil

pinch of sugar

1 tablespoon chopped scallions

1 egg white

1 tablespoon cornstarch

2 tablespoons chopped bamboo shoots*

2 tablespoons chopped water chestnuts

2 cloves garlic, minced

pinch of Chinese five-spice*

1 package shumei skins or gyoza skins*

24 frozen peas

*These items can usually be found in the specialty section of the supermarket, and they are always available at Asian food markets.

Method

· Preheat the oven to 350°F.

· In a large bowl, combine all the ingredients except the shumei skins and peas and mix well. Place 3/4 tablespoon of the mixture in the center of each wrapper.

· Bring up the corners to meet at the top; it will form a "money bag." Place a frozen pea in the center of each shumei and bake for about 10 minutes, or until golden brown.

STUFFED ROASTED CHICKEN WINGS

12 wings

Ingredients for the Marinade

12 whole chicken wings

1/2 teaspoon minced fresh ginger

1/8 cup soy sauce

1/8 cup mirin (sweet rice wine)*

1/2 teaspoon Chinese five-spice*

Ingredients for the Stuffing

1 1/2 cups cooked basmati rice*

1/2 cup chopped raw shrimp

1 egg white

1 teaspoon ground dried shrimp*

1 tablespoon chopped scallions

1/2 teaspoon chopped fresh garlic

1/2 teaspoon minced fresh ginger

2 tablespoons chopped shiitake mushrooms

1/4 teaspoon chopped fresh cilantro

1 1/2 teaspoons fish sauce*

salt and pepper to taste

peanut oil, for frying

1 cup chestnut flour, for frying*

These items can usually be found in the specialty section of the supermarket, and they are always available at Asian food markets.

Method

- With a small knife, create a pocket around each wing bone, leaving the bone in. Combine the rest of the marinade ingredients and marinate the chicken overnight.

- Combine all the stuffing ingredients except the peanut oil and chestnut flour in a bowl. Fill the pockets in the chicken wings with about 1 tablespoon of the stuffing, working the stuffing around the bone. The stuffing should not bulge out of the pocket.

- Heat the peanut oil until very hot in a wok or frying pan. Lightly dredge the wings in the chestnut flour. Fry the wings until they are golden brown, and drain on paper towels.

RICK MOONEN

— Oceana —

After graduating from the Culinary Institute of America in Hyde Park, New York, Rick Moonen began his cooking career in 1980 as a saucier at La Côte Basque in New York City. After two years there, he spent another two years at the renowned New York restaurant Le Cirque. Moonen remained in New York and became executive chef at a number of well-known restaurants, including La Relais, Century Café, and The Water Club. In 1994, Moonen became executive chef and partner at Oceana in Manhattan. Three years later, he and his partners opened Molyvos, a Greek restaurant on Seventh Avenue.

Critics are unanimous in their praise for Moonen's way with seafood, and his restaurants have earned three stars in the *New York Times* and four stars in *Forbes All-Star Eateries in New York*. In 1997, he was named Chef of the Year by *Simply Seafood* magazine.

Moonen is frequently featured in local and national media and often teaches classes for various cooking schools in New York. As a chef and a conference speaker, he has traveled around the world, and he is a director or representative for several companies and products. He also sits on advisory boards for the Culinary Institute of America and the French Culinary Institute in Manhattan. He is active in the leadership of Share Our Strength (SOS), a program promoting hunger prevention and relief, and founded the Chefs Coalition for the Pure Food Campaign.

| MORSEL |

Share Our Strength

People who make their careers out of cooking do so because they enjoy sharing their creativity and the food they make. Many in the profession extend their sharing by helping those who go hungry because of poverty or illness. Chefs routinely participate in charitable programs by donating their time, expertise, and food.

Taste of the Nation is the country's largest culinary benefit to fight hunger. It was originated by Share Our Strength, an organization dedicated to alleviating and preventing hunger, and is supported by Rick Moonen, Jim Coleman, and over six thousand other chefs from coast to coast. Every spring, they prepare their specialties for a variety of Taste of the Nation events in more than one hundred cities. Since 1988, these fundraisers have brought in over $32 million, which Share Our Strength has distributed in grants to more than 450 groups working to fight and prevent hunger.

Share Our Strength has developed a variety of other programs, including Operation Frontline, which coordinates and trains volunteer chefs to teach six-week classes on nutrition, healthy cooking, and food budgeting to individuals at risk of hunger and malnutrition. For more information about Taste of the Nation or Operation Frontline, contact Share Our Strength at (800) 969-4767 or on the Web at www.strength.org.

LOBSTER RAVIOLI IN TOMATO BASIL BROTH

4 servings

Ingredients for the Broth

1/2 cup cleaned, chopped leeks

1/2 cup peeled, chopped onion

2 celery stalks, chopped

4 shallots, peeled and chopped

6 cloves garlic

1 teaspoon black peppercorns

1 16 1/2-ounce can chopped tomatoes, with juice

2 cups white wine

1 cup water

1 tablespoon kosher salt

1 bunch fresh basil, stems only (reserve leaves)

Method for the Broth

· Combine all the ingredients in a stockpot over high heat. When the liquid comes to a boil, reduce the heat and simmer until it is reduced by a third. Strain, discard the solids, and reserve the liquid over low heat in a covered pan.

· Taste the broth, and if the basil flavor is too faint, add more stems and continue cooking on low.

recipe continued on page 137

Ingredients for the Ravioli

1 cup heavy cream

1/2 cup semolina flour

kosher salt and freshly ground white pepper to taste

3 large carrots, peeled

1/4 cup coarsely chopped onion

2 cloves garlic, peeled

3 small shallots, peeled and coarsely chopped

2 cups chicken stock (or canned low-salt chicken broth)

1/3 cup chopped chives

cooked meat from a 1 1/2-pound lobster (cooking method on page 138)

roe from 1 lobster

32 round dumpling wrappers

1 whole egg, beaten

salted water, for cooking

2 fresh plum tomatoes, seeded and diced

Basil Oil (recipe on page 138)

1/3 of the leaves from 1 bunch fresh basil, sliced into thin ribbons (chiffonade), for garnish

Method for the Ravioli

· To make the polenta for the ravioli filling, place the cream in a saucepan and bring it to a simmer over medium-high heat. Add the semolina flour in a slow stream, whisking it into the cream.

· Season with the salt and pepper, combine well, and continue cooking for another 5 minutes. Remove the polenta from the heat and reserve.

· Cut 2 carrots into large chunks and place them in a large stockpot. Add the onion, garlic, shallots, and chicken stock. Put the pot over medium heat and bring to a slow simmer. Reduce the heat to medium-low and cook until the vegetables are tender and the liquid has almost evaporated, about 20 minutes. Transfer the vegetables to a food processor or blender and purée in batches. Allow to cool.

· Combine the vegetable purée with the polenta, fold in the chives, and add the lobster meat and roe to complete the filling.

· Sprinkle semolina flour lightly over a cookie sheet. Working with the dumpling wrappers 2 at a time, flatten them to half their original thickness by rolling them through a pasta machine or by using a rolling pin. Place 1 skin into a ravioli press (or flat on a cutting board).

· Scoop 1 teaspoon of filling into the center, making sure to include some lobster meat. Brush a little beaten egg around the edges, fold the skin over the filling, and seal by pinching the edges with your fingers or pressing with a fork. Place the completed ravioli on the prepared cookie sheet.

· Bring a large pot of salted water to a boil. Return the broth to a simmer. Mince the remaining carrot and add it, along with the tomatoes, to the broth. Put the ravioli in the boiling water and cook for 1 minute. Using a slotted spoon, transfer the ravioli to the tomato broth and cook for 1 more minute.

· Scoop the ravioli out into 4 heated serving bowls. Ladle the broth over each serving and drizzle with Basil Oil. Sprinkle the basil chiffonade over the top and serve.

BASIL OIL

Ingredients

salted water, for boiling

2/3 of the leaves from 1 bunch fresh basil

ice water, for cooling

1 cup vegetable oil

kosher salt

Method

- Bring a pot of salted water to a boil. Briefly dip the basil leaves into the boiling water (about 5 seconds). Immediately plunge the basil into an ice bath to cool. Spread the basil leaves out on paper towels to dry.

- Purée the basil and 1/4 of the vegetable oil in a blender or food processor. With the motor running, slowly add the remaining oil. Taste for seasoning and add at least a pinch of salt. Taste, adjust the seasoning, and reserve.

COOKED LOBSTER

Ingredients

sea or kosher salt

1 lobster (1 1/2 pounds)

Method

- Bring a large stockpot filled with water to a rolling boil. Add 3 to 4 tablespoons sea or kosher salt, and put the lobster in the pot. Cook for approximately 8 minutes, or until the shell turns deep red.

- Remove the lobster to a colander in the sink and allow to drain for 5 minutes. Crack the claws and remove the meat. Open the tail using shears or scissors and remove the meat. Cut the meat into large dices, and hold until ready to use or serve. Remove the roe from the center of the body cavity. Push the roe through a wire mesh sieve and reserve. Discard the legs and body or reserve for another use.

CRISP ATLANTIC SALMON FILLET ON MIXED LENTILS AND MOROCCAN SPICED TOMATO SAUCE WITH HARISSA

4 servings

Ingredients for the Spice Blend

1/2 cup ground coriander

1/4 cup ground cumin

1/2 cup ground fennel seed

2 tablespoons ground cloves

1/4 cup ground cardamom

Method for the Spice Blend

• Combine all the ingredients and mix well. Keep in a glass jar, tightly covered. This will hold its flavor for about 4 weeks.

Ingredients for the Mixed Lentils

1 tablespoon vegetable oil

1 small onion, finely diced

2 cloves garlic, peeled and minced

1/2 cup brown lentils, rinsed

1/2 cup green lentils, rinsed

2 1/2 cups beef broth or water

1 bay leaf

1 teaspoon spice blend (see above)

1 medium carrot, peeled and finely diced

2 tablespoons butter

salt and pepper to taste

Method for the Mixed Lentils

• Put the vegetable oil in a saucepan over medium-high heat. Add the onion and garlic and cook for about 30 seconds. Add the lentils, beef broth or water, bay leaf, and spice blend and bring to a boil.

• Reduce the heat and simmer the lentils for about 25 minutes. Add the carrot and continue to cook for about 10 to 15 more minutes, until the lentils are tender. Remove the bay leaf, blend in the butter, and season to taste with salt and pepper. Keep warm.

recipe continued on page 140

Ingredients for the Moroccan Spiced Tomato Sauce

1/2 cup olive oil

1 cup chopped shallots

1/4 cup chopped fresh garlic

salt and pepper to taste

1   4.875-ounce can harissa (a fiery, hot chili sauce found in Middle Eastern markets)

12 to 15 beefsteak tomatoes, chopped

4 tablespoons spice blend (see page 139), or to taste

Ingredients for the Salmon

2 tablespoons olive oil

spice blend (see page 139), for seasoning

black pepper, for seasoning

4   7-ounce boneless salmon fillets, skin on

1/2 teaspoon butter per fillet

Method for the Moroccan Spiced Tomato Sauce

· Heat the olive oil in a sauté pan over medium heat; add the shallots and garlic. Season with salt and pepper. Sauté the vegetables until they are translucent, about 5 minutes. Add the harissa and stir. Cook for about 3 to 5 minutes. Add the tomatoes and spice blend.

· Purée the mixture in a food processor or blender until the liquid is smooth, and reserve.

Method for the Salmon

· Preheat the oven to 350°F.

· Put the olive oil in a sauté pan over high heat. Season the fish with the spice blend and black pepper.

· When the pan is very hot, add the salmon fillets, skin side down. After about 1 minute, shake the pan to be sure the fish is not sticking. Add the butter in little bits at a time, shaking the pan to incorporate the butter into the oil.

· Place the pan in the oven for about 4 to 5 minutes to roast.

· To serve, place some of the mixed lentils in the center of each plate. Place the salmon on top and drizzle a little of the Moroccan spiced tomato sauce over it.

PEACH MERINGUE WITH CINNAMON-OATMEAL CRUMBLE

4 servings

Ingredients for the Peach Filling

1 pound peaches

1/2 cup sugar

4 egg yolks

Ingredients for the Cinnamon-Oatmeal Crumble

1/2 cup all-purpose flour

1/4 cup sugar

1/2 cup light brown sugar

1 teaspoon cinnamon

1/2 cup oatmeal

2 tablespoons butter, at room temperature

Ingredients for the Meringue

2 egg whites

1/4 cup sugar

1/2 teaspoon vanilla extract

Method for the Peach Filling

- Remove the pits from the peaches and cut into chunks.

- Place the peaches in a saucepan, mix with the sugar, and cover. Stew the peaches over very low heat until very soft, about 15 to 20 minutes. Be sure to stir every 5 minutes so that the mixture does not scorch.

- Pour the peach mixture into a strainer and let the juice run into a bowl. Return the juice to the pot and cook until it is reduced by half.

- In the meantime, place the solids in a food processor and purée until smooth. Add the reduced juice and mix until combined. Stir the peach mixture into the egg yolks slowly, so that the heat of the peaches does not cook the egg yolks.

Method for the Cinnamon-Oatmeal Crumble

- Combine all the ingredients in a bowl and rub together until the mixture resembles the size of small peas. Set aside.

Method for the Meringue

- Whip the egg whites to stiff peaks and add the sugar, then the vanilla, in steady streams while whipping. Set aside.

Method for Assembling the Peach Meringues

- Preheat the oven to 325°F.

- Pour the peach filling into 4 individual baking dishes. The dishes should be no more than 1 inch in height. Leave a 1/4-inch margin at the top.

- Sprinkle a layer of the cinnamon-oatmeal crumble on top of the filling, place the dishes on a cookie sheet, and reserve.

- Spoon about 1/2 cup of meringue on top of each peach crumble. Using the flat side of a rubber spatula, touch the meringue and lift it up to form spikes. Place the dishes in the oven and bake for about 20 minutes. Serve warm.

CELEBRATING THANKSGIVING

The idea for the first Thanksgiving was loosely based on the European harvest festival, but ever since the Pilgrims sat down with their Indian neighbors in gratitude, the celebration has symbolized the many bounties of this land. The traditions of that first feast are reenacted each year as Americans revel in their appreciation of life in this country.

Modern Thanksgiving dinners evoke the spirit of the original but have broadened to include ingredients from different American regions and around the world. Most of the herbs and spices used to flavor Thanksgiving dishes today were not available in early Plymouth, and many fruits, nuts, and vegetables have been added to the banquet over the years. The original menu, drawn up by Plymouth governor William Bradford, included oysters, eel, and venison. No mention was made of cranberries or pumpkins, and if turkey was served (historians continue to debate the issue), the Pilgrims' wild fowl would have borne little resemblance to the plump, juicy birds that crown today's holiday tables.

The Pilgrims were the first Americans to adapt to new foods and cooking techniques that were better suited to their changing needs and tastes in the New World. Generations after that first multicultural meal, the Thanksgiving repast is a harmony of traditional ingredients and dynamic new influences inspired by the many people who now call this country home.

MORSEL

The Making of a Holiday

The Pilgrims and the Wampanoag Indians may have celebrated the first Thanksgiving in 1623, but it was not a national affair until President George Washington proclaimed a day of thanksgiving on November 26, 1789. Up to that time, thanksgiving celebrations were local parties in the years when harvests were particularly good. Washington only decreed one official Thanksgiving, and it was up to subsequent presidents to name their own dates and reasons for celebrating the event, such as the end of the War of 1812.

Thanksgiving was made an annual, national holiday by President Abraham Lincoln, who might not have taken the initiative had it not been for a lady from Philadelphia named Sarah Josepha Hale. Best known as the editor of the national magazine Godey's Lady's Book and also as the author of "Mary Had a Little Lamb," she and her readers crusaded for the holiday by flooding Congress and the White House with letters and petitions. President Lincoln saw the merit in her suggestion and the public support behind it. In 1863, he proclaimed the last Thursday in November the nation's Thanksgiving Day.

MORSEL

Cranberries

One of only three fruits indigenous to this continent (the others are blueberries and Concord grapes), cranberries were enjoyed by Native Americans for centuries before any European ever tasted one. The Indians did not make a sauce of the berries, but rather dried them by placing them in layers between hot rocks in tightly woven baskets. The dried berries were easy to pack and were ideal for tribes that were always on the go.

European settlers quickly became cranberry fans, but they added the sweetness of honey or sugar and began the tradition of making the berries into a sauce or relish for meat. Sailors out of New England seaports stored cranberries on their ships because they were known to prevent scurvy (due to the large amount of vitamin C they contain), and their citric acid helped to preserve them for long voyages. Their portability made cranberries the first North American fruit to go to market in Europe, where they were labeled "Cape Cod berries" and fetched top dollar.

CURRIED ACORN SQUASH SOUP

4 servings

Ingredients

1 acorn squash, halved and seeded

1/4 cup European-style butter (such as Keller's)

1 tablespoon chopped fresh garlic

1 cup chopped onion

2 teaspoons curry powder

1 teaspoon ground cumin

1/8 teaspoon ground allspice

2 cups chicken stock

1/2 cup milk

salt and pepper to taste

2 tablespoons chopped chives

Method

• Preheat the oven to 350°F. Spray a baking sheet with nonstick cooking spray.

• Place the squash cut side down on the baking sheet. Bake until soft, about 40 minutes. Scoop out the squash pulp and discard the skin.

• In a large saucepan, melt the butter and add the garlic, onion, curry powder, cumin, and allspice. Sauté until the onion is tender, about 10 minutes. Purée the squash with the onion mixture and the chicken stock using a food processor, blender, or hand blender.

• Pour the purée back into the saucepan, add the milk, and bring to a boil. Reduce the heat and simmer for about 10 minutes, stirring occasionally. Season with salt and pepper, and stir in the chives.

ROAST TURKEY AND GRAVY WITH APRICOT AND HERB STUFFING

8 to 12 servings of turkey

Ingredients

6 tablespoons European-style butter
(such as Keller's), at room temperature

1 clove garlic, chopped

1 large shallot, chopped

2 teaspoons chopped fresh thyme

2 teaspoons chopped fresh sage

1 12- to 14-pound turkey,
neck and giblets reserved

salt and pepper to taste

5 cups chicken stock

1 1/3 cups dry white vermouth

2 bay leaves

6 tablespoons all-purpose flour

1/2 cup chopped fresh parsley

Apricot and Herb Stuffing (recipe on page 147)

Method

· Mix the first 5 ingredients in a bowl and keep at room temperature.

· Preheat the oven to 425°F.

· Place the turkey in a roasting pan and pull the skin away from the turkey. Using your hands, rub the butter mixture all over the meat under the skin. Season with salt and pepper. Place the neck and giblets and 2 cups of the chicken stock around the turkey in the pan.

· Roast the turkey for about 30 minutes. Reduce the heat to 325°F, and continue to cook until the internal temperature registers 175°F on a meat thermometer. Baste about every 30 minutes. The cooking time should be about 3 1/2 hours.

· When done, transfer the turkey to a platter and cover with foil. Allow to stand for 30 minutes.

· To make the gravy, pour the pan juices into a cup, discarding the neck and the giblets. Spoon the fat from the surface of the juices and place the fat in a small saucepan.

· Place the roasting pan across two burners of the stove over medium-high heat. Add the vermouth, the reserved juices, and the remaining chicken stock to the roasting pan and scrape the browned bits from the bottom. Add the bay leaves and cook for about 5 minutes.

· Meanwhile, heat the fat in the saucepan and whisk in the flour. Cook for about 3 minutes, or until the mixture is pale golden brown. Add the liquid from the roasting pan to the saucepan with the flour mixture, whisking all the time. Allow the gravy to reduce until it coats the back of a spoon. Season with salt, pepper, and the parsley. Discard the bay leaf. Serve with Apricot and Herb Stuffing.

APRICOT AND HERB STUFFING

Ingredients

4 tablespoons European-style butter (such as Keller's)

1 1/2 cups chopped onion

2 tablespoons chopped fresh garlic

1/2 cup chopped celery

1/4 cup chopped scallions

1/4 cup chopped fresh parsley

4 cups dried bread cubes

1/3 cup dried apricots, roughly chopped

1/2 cup chopped walnuts

1 teaspoon dried basil

1 teaspoon dried oregano

1 teaspoon dried sage

1/2 cup chicken stock

salt and pepper to taste

Method

· Preheat the oven to 325°F.

· Heat the butter in a large sauté pan. Sauté the onion and garlic for about 5 minutes over medium heat. Add the celery and scallions and sauté for 2 more minutes.

· In a large bowl, mix the onion mixture with all the remaining ingredients. Place the stuffing in a well-greased baking dish and bake for 1 hour.

MINTED GREEN BEANS AND PEARL ONIONS IN A BROWN BUTTER SAUCE

6 to 8 servings

Ingredients

1 pint pearl onions

2 pounds cleaned green beans

1/4 cup European-style butter (such as Keller's)

1/4 cup chopped fresh mint

1 tablespoon chopped fresh tarragon

salt and pepper to taste

Method

· Bring 2 quarts of water to a boil. Add the pearl onions and cook for 2 to 3 minutes. Remove the onions from the water with a slotted spoon and cool in a bowl of ice water.

· Add the beans to the boiling water and cook for about 2 minutes, or until tender but not mushy. Remove from the water and cool in the ice water. Peel the onions.

· Melt the butter in a medium sauté pan. Add the onions and cook until the butter begins to brown. Add the beans, mint, and tarragon and sauté until heated through, about 1 minute. Season with salt and pepper.

CRANBERRY-ORANGE RELISH WITH WALNUTS

1 quart

Ingredients

2 large oranges

3 cups fresh cranberries

1 cup sugar

1/2 cup rice wine vinegar

1/2 cup walnuts, coarsely chopped

Method

• Peel and segment the oranges, and remove all seeds.

• Combine all the ingredients in a medium-size saucepan and simmer over medium heat for about 5 minutes. Remove from the heat and allow to cool. Serve chilled.

PUMPKIN CRÈME BRÛLÉE

6 servings

Ingredients

5 egg yolks

1 1/2 cups unsweetened pumpkin purée

1/2 cup sugar

4 teaspoons vanilla extract

1 teaspoon ground cinnamon

1/2 teaspoon ground ginger

1/2 teaspoon ground cloves

1/4 teaspoon grated nutmeg

3 cups heavy cream

1/2 cup light brown sugar

Method

• Preheat the oven to 325°F. Lightly butter 6 individual ramekins or brûlée molds.

• In a mixing bowl, whisk the egg yolks slowly into the pumpkin purée. Whisk in the sugar, vanilla, and spices. Set aside.

• In a large saucepan, bring the cream to a boil. Slowly whisk the cream into the egg and pumpkin mixture. Divide the mix among the ramekins.

• Place the molds in a baking pan that has 3- to 4-inch sides. Pour enough boiling water into the baking pan so that it comes halfway up the sides of the ramekins. Bake in the oven for about 1 hour, or until golden but not firm. Remove from the pan and allow to cool. (The crème brûlée will continue to thicken as it cools.) Cover and refrigerate until very cold.

• Heat the broiler and set a rack as high as it will go in the oven.

• Evenly coat the tops of the brûlées with a thin layer of the brown sugar. Brown the brûlées under the broiler for 30 seconds to 3 minutes, or until the tops become a rich, dark brown. Serve warm.

JACK McDAVID

— Jack's Firehouse and The Down Home Diner —

Instead of a toque and a chef's uniform, Jack McDavid brandishes a baseball hat imprinted with "Save the Farm" and a pair of overalls as he oversees the hectic pace in his two highly successful restaurants in Philadelphia. His attire reflects his Virginia roots and a dedication to the agricultural quality still provided by family farms.

McDavid became interested in cooking while he was studying accounting and working his way toward a law degree at the University of Virginia. His after-school bookkeeping job at a local restaurant tempted him to try his hand in the kitchen. When nearby Monticello needed a chef, McDavid was picked for the job and found himself serving the likes of Queen Elizabeth II, Jimmy Carter, Anwar Sadat, and Menachem Begin.

The enthusiastic response to his cooking prompted him to change career courses and to further his culinary expertise. He learned the techniques, timing, and art of the culinary profession by working with a variety of chefs. When he had mastered all aspects of the kitchen, he was hired by Le Bec-Fin, the five-star Philadelphia restaurant owned by chef Georges Perrier, who encouraged McDavid to experiment with food.

In 1987, McDavid opened his first restaurant, The Down Home Diner, in Philadelphia's Reading Terminal Market. Decorated in full diner regalia, Down Home offers the freshest food available in a wide variety of American regional styles. McDavid opened Jack's Firehouse in 1989, fulfilling his dream to operate a restaurant serving "haute country" cuisine.

McDavid's emphasis on garden-fresh produce in his cooking has led him to invest in area greenhouses to ensure a steady supply of perfect vegetables and herbs. He also operates a summer kitchen in a local barn, where he bottles 40,000 quarts of specialty sauces, condiments, and pickles that are served in his restaurants year-round.

> ## MORSEL
>
> ### Demiglace
>
> Demiglace is a savory beef sauce that is the basis for many elegant preparations. The main component of traditional demiglace is basic brown sauce (also called espagnole sauce), which is made with a rich meat stock, sautéed mixed vegetables, a brown roux, and herbs. This brown sauce is combined with beef stock and Madeira wine or sherry, then slowly cooked until reduced by half (hence its name) and thick enough to coat a spoon.
>
> The process of making demiglace is time-consuming and usually undertaken only in restaurants. This rich sauce base is available in specialty shops, but for the home cook an acceptable substitute is canned beef stock reduced by half.

ROASTED CORN AND RASPBERRY SOUP

4 servings

Ingredients

12 ears of corn, unshucked

1 tablespoon chopped fresh basil

salt and pepper to taste

1 quart raspberries

1 fresh jalapeño pepper

2 tablespoons honey

corn flakes, for garnish

Method

- Place the corn on a medium-hot grill and roast for about 9 minutes. Turn it over and roast for an additional 9 minutes. Allow the ears to cool until they are comfortable to handle. Shuck the corn, then cut the kernels off the cob and scrape the cob to milk the corn.

- Place the corn, the corn milk, and the basil in a blender and purée. Season with salt and pepper to taste. Pour the purée into a saucepan and heat to a simmer. Cover the pan and keep the purée hot over low heat.

- Clean the blender. Purée the raspberries, jalapeño, and honey in the blender. Strain this mixture, pour it into a saucepan, and reduce the volume by half over low heat.

- Divide the hot corn purée among 4 soup bowls. Swirl the raspberry reduction into each bowl of corn soup. Garnish with the corn flakes.

RUBBED FRONTIER COWBOY STEAK
WITH BOURBON AND CORN SAUCE

2 to 4 servings

Ingredients for the Rub

2 ounces salt

4 ounces brown sugar

1 ounce black pepper

2 ounces ground dried chipotle pepper

2 16-ounce cowboy steaks (bone-on ribeyes)

Ingredients for the Sauce

1 teaspoon minced shallots

1 tablespoon vegetable oil

1/4 cup bourbon

1 cup demiglace or reduced beef stock

3 ounces fresh corn kernels, or about 2 ears' worth

salt and pepper to taste

chive blossoms, for garnish

Method

- Combine all the ingredients for the rub and spread on both sides of each steak. Allow the meat to stand for about 15 minutes. Heat the grill and sear the steak for 4 minutes. Turn the steak and sear the other side for 4 more minutes, or until the steak is cooked as desired.

- Sauté the shallots in the vegetable oil. Remove the pan from the heat and add the bourbon. Place the pan back on the heat and ignite the sauce with a match. When the flame dies down, stir in the demiglace or beef stock and the corn. Season with salt and pepper and pour the sauce over the steak. Garnish with the chive blossoms.

GRILLED FRUIT WITH MANGO CREAM

4 servings

Ingredients for the Mango Cream

1 overripe mango

1/2 overripe banana

1 tablespoon honey

6 ounces heavy cream, whipped to soft peaks

4 ounces sour cream

Ingredients for the Grilled Fruit

1 pineapple, peeled and cut into 1-inch slices

2 pears, cored and cut into 1/2-inch slices

1 apple, cored and cut into 1/2-inch slices

1 pint strawberries, halved

1 mango, peeled and cut into 1/2-inch slices

1/2 bunch mint

Method

- Blend the overripe mango and the banana with the honey. Fold the whipped cream and sour cream into the blended fruit and set aside.

- Preheat the grill to medium heat.

- Grill the pineapple, pear, and apple slices until they begin to brown. Turn them over, add the strawberries, and brown the second side.

- Arrange a platter with the mango slices around the outside. Place the pineapple, pear, and apple slices in the center and place the strawberries on top.

- Place dollops of the mango cream around the platter and garnish with the mint.

A CHRISTMAS FEAST

The English tradition of celebrating with succulent roast beef and Yorkshire pudding presents a delicious alternative to turkey and ham for Christmas dinner. In Britain, meals of this kind have been served for hundreds of years on Sundays and other special occasions when regular fare simply will not do. Visitors to the country have long raved about the perfect touch the British seem to possess in the preparation of a carefully selected roast or "joint." It was not until the first great cattle roundups in the American West that England lost its title as the world's largest beef producer and consumer.

Yorkshire pudding rounds out a roast beef meal with Dickensian flair. This savory dish, named after a northern English county, was first prepared as a thick batter poured into the pan underneath the roast as it cooked on a spit. The pudding was flavored with meat juices that dripped into the batter. First printed in England in 1747, the recipe has been reversed in modern times so that the drippings are poured into the bottom of the pudding pan before the batter is added. The pudding rises like a soufflé as it cooks.

The first gingerbread men were made in the likeness of guests visiting Queen Elizabeth I, who employed a full-time gingerbread maker. The molds became so complicated that sculptors were required to make them, and some gingerbread creations were adorned in full color with gold leaf designs.

Gingerbread came to America when the Pilgrims packed their favorite recipes and took them aboard the *Mayflower*. It was prized as a standard ration in the army of George Washington, whose own mother was noted for her particularly spicy version. Five different gingerbread recipes appeared in the first American cookbook, *American Cookery*, published in 1796. It was not long before Americans had adopted the tradition of serving roast beef, Yorkshire pudding, and gingerbread at their own celebrations.

MORSEL

Ginger

Ginger has been so popular in cooking for so many thousands of years that the plant no longer appears in the wild anywhere in the world. There is only one species of ginger, and it is believed to have first sprouted in tropical Asia, but its origin is somewhat mysterious since domestication of the plant predates written history.

The earliest recorded use of ginger was in China, where food has always been prepared with the health benefits of its ingredients in mind. The ancient Chinese believed ginger was bursting with medicinal goodness, and they prescribed ginger-laced dishes for everything from colds to leprosy. Beyond its curative powers, ginger was believed to cleanse the spirit, and Confucius was reported to have eaten the spice daily. The Chinese were also the first of many cultures to use ginger to cure meat and to mask the rankness of leftovers.

With all it had going for it, it is no wonder that when the first spice traders brought it to India and further west, ginger became a star in ancient kitchens. Both fresh and dried forms became integral parts of almost all Asian and Middle Eastern cuisines, and they remain so today. In Greece, Hippocrates endorsed ginger's medicinal qualities, but in Rome it was preferred for its flavor. Romans created the earliest form of gingerbread by including the spice in their bread recipes. They discovered it not only added a zippy taste but acted as a preservative as well. Roman legions introduced gingerbread, along with the spice, to Northern Europe, and both became important in medieval cookery.

STANDING RIB ROAST

6 to 8 servings

Ingredients

2 tablespoons Dijon mustard

2 cloves garlic, chopped

2 shallots, chopped

1 teaspoon chopped fresh thyme

1 teaspoon chopped fresh rosemary

1 teaspoon chopped fresh oregano

1   8- or 9-pound beef rib roast, bone in

3 onions, peeled and cut into 2-inch chunks

2 carrots, cut into 1-inch chunks

salt and pepper to taste

Method

- Preheat the oven to 450°F.

- Combine the mustard, garlic, shallots, and herbs and rub on the roast. Place the onions and carrots on the bottom of a large roasting pan and place the roast on top of them. Season the roast to taste with salt and pepper.

- Place the pan in the oven and roast for 20 minutes. Reduce the temperature to 300°F and roast for about 2 more hours, or until the internal temperature is 115°F. At this temperature the roast will be rare in the center.

- Remove the roast from the oven and allow to stand for about 20 minutes in a warm place before carving.

YORKSHIRE PUDDING WITH GOAT CHEESE

6 to 8 servings

Ingredients

1 cup all-purpose flour

pinch of grated nutmeg

1/2 teaspoon salt

1/2 cup milk, at room temperature

2 eggs, beaten and at room temperature

1/2 cup water, at room temperature

2 tablespoons fat drippings from the roasting pan, or 2 tablespoons oil

1/4 cup crumbled goat cheese

1 tablespoon chopped parsley

Method

- Preheat the oven to 400°F.

- Combine the flour, nutmeg, and salt in a mixing bowl. Stir in the milk and beat until light and airy. Stir in the eggs and water and beat until well combined.

- Coat the inside of an ovenproof dish with the fat drippings or oil. Pour the batter into the dish and crumble the goat cheese over the top. Place the dish in the oven and bake for 20 minutes.

- Reduce the temperature to 350°F and continue baking for 5 to 10 more minutes, until puffy and golden brown. Sprinkle the parsley over the top and serve while still hot.

BRAISED RED CABBAGE

6 to 8 servings

Ingredients

3 pounds red cabbage, cored and shredded

1 1/2 cups beef stock

1/2 cup light brown sugar

1/2 cup rice wine vinegar

2 shallots, chopped

2 cloves garlic, chopped

1/2 teaspoon caraway seeds

4 tablespoons European-style butter (such as Keller's)

2 bay leaves

salt and pepper to taste

Method

- Combine all the ingredients except the salt and pepper in a 10-quart pot and bring to a boil. Reduce the heat, cover, and simmer over low heat, stirring occasionally, for 1 hour. Season with salt and pepper and serve hot.

CREAMY PEARL ONIONS AND PEAS

6 to 8 servings

Ingredients

2 1/2 pounds pearl onions

2 cups chicken stock

3 tablespoons European-style butter
(such as Keller's)

1 teaspoon chopped fresh garlic

1/2 teaspoon turmeric

6 tablespoons all-purpose flour

1 cup half-and-half

1/4 cup dry sherry

1 pound frozen peas

1/8 teaspoon ground nutmeg

2 tablespoons chopped fresh parsley

salt and pepper to taste

1 tablespoon grated Parmesan cheese

Method

• Preheat the oven to 375°F.

• Bring a pot of water to a boil, add the onions, and cook for about 30 seconds. Remove the onions from the hot water and cool in an ice water bath. Peel the onions.

• Bring the chicken stock to a simmer in a saucepan. In a small frying pan, melt the butter, add the garlic and turmeric, and sauté until fragrant. Add the flour, stir, and cook together to make a golden roux. Do not brown.

• Add the roux to the simmering stock and whisk until smooth and thickened. Stir in the half-and-half and sherry and simmer for 2 minutes. Add the peas, nutmeg, and parsley. Season with salt and pepper.

• Combine the onions and the stock mixture and place in an ovenproof baking dish. Sprinkle the Parmesan cheese over the top and bake for about 15 minutes.

GINGERBREAD COOKIES

8 to 10 large cookies

Ingredients

3/4 cup European-style butter (such as Keller's), at room temperature

1 cup light brown sugar

1/2 cup dark molasses

1 tablespoon fresh lemon juice

4 1/2 cups all-purpose flour

1 1/2 teaspoons baking soda

1/4 teaspoon ground cloves

2 1/2 teaspoons ground ginger

1 1/2 teaspoons allspice

1/4 teaspoon ground cardamom

3 tablespoons cold water

Method

- Preheat the oven to 350°F.

- In the bowl of an electric mixer, cream the butter and brown sugar together for 5 minutes. Add the molasses and lemon juice and beat until well combined.

- Combine all the dry ingredients in a separate mixing bowl. Add the dry ingredients to the butter mixture and blend until combined.

- Add the water and mix until a dough is formed and holds together. Cover and refrigerate for 1 hour. Roll out the dough to 1/4 inch thick on a lightly floured surface. Cut figures out of the dough with a gingerbread man cookie cutter. Arrange the cookies on a well-greased cookie sheet and bake for 15 to 20 minutes, or until golden brown.

THREE SUPERB CHEFS, THREE ELEGANT DESSERTS

— François Payard —

François Payard is a third-generation French pastry chef who began learning the art of pastry in his grandfather's bakery on the Riviera. After honing his skills in classic pastry making with his family, Payard moved to Paris, where he learned the artistic refinement of transforming traditional desserts into exquisite plated presentations.

Payard's expertise earned him positions in some of the finest kitchens in France, notably the three-star Michelin-rated La Tour d'Argent and Lucas Carton. His desire to travel brought him to New York City, where he started his American career as pastry chef at Le Bernadin. In 1993, Payard joined Daniel Boulud to open Restaurant Daniel, also in New York, where he delighted guests with his fanciful creations.

The James Beard Foundation named Payard Pastry Chef of the Year in 1995, in recognition of his accent on flavor combined with a unique sense of pastry design. Fulfilling a lifelong dream, Payard opened Patisserie in 1997, where he offers confections that would have made his grandfather proud.

— Robert Bennett —

Robert Bennett has been passionate about cooking since his childhood in Lynchburg, Virginia, where he experimented in his family kitchen and took after-school jobs in area restaurants. After high school, he earned a degree from the New England Culinary Institute, where he received a Distinguished Graduate Award and was asked to remain as the executive pastry instructor. During his tenure, Bennett was invited to President Reagan's second inaugural as guest pastry chef. For the occasion, he created a gigantic cake replicating Capitol Hill that served 44,000 people.

After three semesters of teaching, Bennett was offered a position as executive pastry chef/consultant at the Jumby Bay Resort in Antigua, West Indies. In 1987, he took a position at the renowned Philadelphia restaurant Le Bec-Fin, where he was soon named head pastry chef. In 1989, Bennett represented the United States in the premier World Cup Pastry Championship in Lyon, France; his team took fifth place.

In 1992, Bennett co-founded the Philadelphia Pastry Society, which comprises approximately 120 members. He is active in numerous fundraisers and donates desserts to more than thirty charities each year. Bennett was recently appointed to the board of directors of the North American Pastry Chefs Association, a nationwide organization made up of the country's top pastry chefs.

— John Gallagher —

John Gallagher is a graduate of the Culinary Institute of America and has attended the Cocoa Barry Pastry and Confection School. He has served as pastry chef at La Panetière Pastry Shop and the Hotel atop the Bellevue, both located in Philadelphia, and at The Mansion at Main Street, in Voorhees, New Jersey. He has also worked at New York's Grand Hyatt Hotel and Essex Park South.

In 1995, Gallagher became a member of the faculty at the Restaurant School in Philadelphia, and in 1997 he was appointed the school's executive pastry chef. While he teaches his students the techniques and precision required in baking, he explains his philosophy about being a pastry chef: "Baking is the first thing your patrons encounter when they sit down [bread or rolls], and the last thing they experience before they leave your restaurant. So you are the one who will set the tone for the whole meal…and you must set the standard that the rest of the meal must live up to."

Gallagher tells his students to never be satisfied with just "good," and he invites them to share his passion for always trying to reach the next level of perfection. He reminds them to hone their basic skills and never compromise standards throughout the long hours and heavy work it takes to become a pastry chef. "The glamour," he promises, "will come when you're ready."

BANANA TART — Chef François Payard

8 servings

Ingredients for the Tart Crust

8 tablespoons clarified butter

4 sheets phyllo dough

3/4 cup (3 ounces) salted cashews, crushed

Ingredients for the White Chocolate Mousse

1 cup chopped white chocolate

3/4 cup whipped cream

Ingredients for the Banana Filling

3 tablespoons whole butter

1 tablespoon sugar

4 bananas, cut into 1/2-inch pieces

3 tablespoons dark rum

Ingredients for the Passion Fruit Sauce

1 cup passion fruit purée

1 cup half-and-half

4 egg yolks

1/3 cup sugar

Method for the Tart Crust

- Preheat the oven to 375°F.

- Line a cookie sheet with parchment paper and brush with clarified butter. Place 1 sheet of phyllo dough over the parchment paper, brush with clarified butter, sprinkle with cashews, and cover with a second sheet of phyllo dough. Flatten both layers with the back of a heavy pot. Cover with a third sheet of phyllo, brush with clarified butter, add the fourth sheet of phyllo, and flatten again with a pot.

- Cut into rounds with a 5-inch circle cutter. Place each round inside a 4-inch tart mold or ramekin, pressing the dough against the sides to form a tart shell. Chill the shells in the refrigerator for 10 minutes, then bake for 6 to 7 minutes, or until golden brown.

Method for the White Chocolate Mousse

- Melt the white chocolate in the top half of a double boiler to 120°F and set aside. In a cold mixing bowl over ice, whip the cream to a thick ribbon consistency and fold in the melted chocolate.

- Line a cookie sheet with parchment paper, spread the chocolate mixture evenly over the pan, and freeze until hardened. Using a 4-inch circle cutter, cut out 8 chocolate circles, and return to the freezer until ready to use.

Method for the Banana Filling

- In a sauté pan, melt the butter, add the sugar, and combine well. Add the bananas, pour in the rum, and ignite (flambé) the bananas, cooking until the flame subsides.

Method for the Passion Fruit Sauce

- Bring the fruit purée and half-and-half to a boil in a saucepan. In a mixing bowl, beat the egg yolks with the sugar until smooth, and add to the fruit mixture. Cook over medium heat for 10 minutes, strain through a fine sieve, and cool in the refrigerator.

recipe continued on page 162

Method for Assembling the Tarts

- Using a ring approximately 4 inches wide and 2 inches high, layer the ingredients in the following order: 1 phyllo crust circle, 1 white chocolate circle, 1 phyllo crust circle, 1 layer of cooked banana slices. Repeat with remaining ingredients to make 8 servings. Garnish with the passion fruit sauce and ice cream.

GÂTEAU AU CHOCOLAT LE BEC-FIN — Chef Robert Bennett

makes 3 8-inch cakes

Ingredients for the Cakes

10 egg yolks

3/4 cup plus 6 tablespoons sugar

1 tablespoon water

7/8 cup pastry flour

10 tablespoons Dutch process cocoa powder

2 1/4 teaspoons baking powder

10 egg whites

1/2 teaspoon cream of tartar

Ingredients for the Syrup

2 cups sugar

2 cups water

1 cup dark rum

Ingredients for the Chocolate Buttercream

5 eggs

3/4 cup sugar

3/4 pound semisweet chocolate, melted and cooled

9 tablespoons unsalted butter, softened

Method for the Cakes

- Preheat the oven to 350°F.

- Butter and flour 3 8-inch cake pans. Combine the egg yolks, 3/4 cup of the sugar, and the water and beat on high speed until light and pale yellow.

- Sift together the flour, cocoa, and baking powder and set aside. In a clean, dry bowl, beat the egg whites and cream of tartar until soft peaks form. Sprinkle in the remaining 6 tablespoons of sugar, then beat again until stiff and glossy.

- Fold 1/2 of the egg whites into the egg yolk mixture. Fold in the dry ingredients, then fold in the remaining egg whites. Divide the batter among the 3 prepared pans. Bake for 30 minutes, or until the cakes pull away from the sides of the pan. Allow to cool for 10 minutes, then invert the cakes onto racks to cool completely.

Method for the Syrup

- In a small pan, bring the sugar and water to a boil. When clear, remove from the heat and stir in the rum. Let the mixture cool to room temperature.

Method for the Chocolate Buttercream

- Whisk the eggs and sugar in the top of a double boiler set over simmering water until they are very warm. Pour this mixture into a mixing bowl and whip at high speed until cooled and light. Reduce the speed and

recipe continued on page 163

Ingredients for the Chocolate Fans

6 ounces semisweet chocolate couverture, finely chopped (see Chef's Tip)

1 tablespoon peanut oil

confectioners' sugar, for dusting

3 to 4 ounces shaved chocolate, for garnish

CHEF'S TIP:
Chocolate couverture is professional-quality coating chocolate that is very glossy. Couverture has a greater percentage of butterfat than other forms of chocolate, which allows it to form thinner and harder shells or layers. This specific kind of cooking chocolate can be found in specialty cooking stores.

pour in the melted chocolate. Increase the speed to medium and add the butter. Beat until light and fluffy, then set aside.

Method for the Chocolate Fans

• Melt the chopped chocolate with the peanut oil. Have ready 2 flat baking sheets. Warm them slightly in the oven, then remove. Using a flat metal spatula, spread the chocolate thinly over the backs of both sheets, dividing it evenly. Refrigerate until set, about 15 minutes.

• Remove 1 tray at a time from the refrigerator. Line another sheet with parchment paper. Allow the chocolate to warm slightly, about 3 minutes. Test the chocolate by scraping up an edge of it with a straight-edged metal spatula. The chocolate should form wavy fans. If the chocolate breaks instead of fanning, it is too cold. If it will not come off the tray, it is too warm.

• When ready, gently scrape up 3 to 4 inches of chocolate, using your free hand to lightly hold onto the edge of the chocolate fan. (This will encourage the other side to pleat freely.) As you finish each fan, place it on the parchment-lined baking sheet and refrigerate. (If storing, transfer to an airtight, covered container and refrigerate for up to 2 days.)

Method for Assembling the Cakes

• Using a long, serrated knife, split each cake into 3 layers. For each cake, place 1 layer on a cardboard cake circle or a cake platter. Brush generously with the syrup. Spread a thin layer of chocolate buttercream over the cake, making sure to spread all the way to the edge. Top with a second cake layer, brush with syrup, and spread with buttercream, repeating until all 3 layers are assembled. Coat the entire cake with buttercream and garnish the sides with shaved chocolate.

• Arrange the fans with their pointed sides in to make a circle around the outside edge of the cake. Then, arrange more fans to make a second circle, forming a point in the center of the cake. (The entire top of the cake should be covered with layered chocolate fans.) Dust the top of the cake with confectioners' sugar and serve.

FRANGIPAN CAKE — Chef John Gallagher

8 to 10 servings

Ingredients

15 ounces almond paste

9 eggs

12 ounces (1 1/2 cups) butter

12 ounces (1 1/2 cups) sugar

1 tablespoon vanilla

1 teaspoon salt

4 ounces sifted cake flour

Method

- Preheat the oven to 350°F.

- Using an electric mixer with a paddle attachment, beat the almond paste with 2 eggs until smooth. Add the butter and sugar and beat until light and fluffy, scraping the bowl often.

- Slowly add the remaining eggs in 3 stages, scraping between each stage. Add the vanilla and salt. Add the flour and stir until it is incorporated.

- Pour the batter into a lightly greased 9-inch cake pan and bake until the cake is golden brown and springs back when touched.

PATRICK O'CONNELL

— The Inn at Little Washington –

A native of Washington, D.C., Patrick O'Connell got his first taste of the culinary world by working in a neighborhood restaurant after school at the age of fifteen. Later, as a student of speech and drama at Catholic University of America, he found himself in a restaurant once again, waiting on tables to finance his education. After spending a year traveling in Europe, he decided that the "living theater" of the restaurant business was more compelling than an acting career, and he decided to become a chef.

As soon as he took command of the kitchen, he knew he had found his calling. Today, O'Connell is executive chef at The Inn at Little Washington, which in 1989 became the first establishment in the United States to earn five stars from the *Mobil Travel Guide*. A member of the Paris-based Relais & Châteaux Association, the restaurant also achieved a five-diamond rating from the American Automobile Association and the top national rating in the Zagat hotel survey.

In 1992, the James Beard Foundation voted O'Connell the best chef in the Mid-Atlantic region, and went on to name The Inn at Little Washington Restaurant of the Year in 1993. O'Connell is an original member of Who's Who in Food in America. Not surprisingly, he is also the author of the cookbook *The Inn at Little Washington: A Consuming Passion*.

MORSEL

Figs

As the Old Testament can attest, figs have figured in mankind's diet for at least three thousand years. They grew in the hanging gardens of Babylon and were cultivated by the Phoenicians and ancient Egyptians. Their predominance in Mediterranean cuisines gives them an exotic quality, and Americans tend to think of them as somewhat foreign. However, Spanish missionaries began to grow fig trees in California as early as the sixteenth century, and the first American fig crops were harvested about the same time the fruit was introduced in Elizabethan England. Today, the United States is the world's third-largest fig producer, with 99 percent of the American crop grown near Fresno, California.

The multiseeded fruit is most commonly eaten dried, but modern shipping methods are increasing the availability of figs right off the tree. Fresh figs offer a delicately sweet flavor that pairs beautifully with other foods. The little, balloon-shaped fruits are nutritious, too—they offer more dietary fiber than bran flakes, are a significant source of calcium, and ounce for ounce contain more potassium than bananas.

CHILLED GRILLED BLACK MISSION FIGS WITH VIRGINIA COUNTRY HAM AND LIME CREAM

4 servings

Ingredients

12 fresh Black Mission figs, sliced in half lengthwise

2 tablespoons olive oil

1 tablespoon sugar

1 teaspoon ground cinnamon

1/2 cup heavy cream

1/4 cup fresh lime juice

pinch of freshly grated nutmeg

2 limes

6 ounces Virginia ham, thinly sliced

4 teaspoons snipped fresh chives

Method

• Preheat a gas grill or a broiler.

• Brush the figs with the olive oil. Combine the sugar and cinnamon in a small bowl and sprinkle it over the figs.

• If using a grill, lay the figs flat side down on the grill rack. Heat them for 2 to 3 minutes, until they soften but still hold their shape.

• If using a broiler, place the figs flat side up on a lightly oiled baking sheet and broil them as close to the heating element as possible for 2 to 3 minutes. Remove the figs from the heat and allow to cool to room temperature. (The figs may be prepared a day in advance and kept refrigerated, but their flavor is far superior when they are served at room temperature.)

• Pour the cream into the bowl of an electric mixer and whip until it begins to form soft peaks. Slowly add the lime juice and nutmeg, blending until the mixture has the consistency of a thick sauce. Place the cream in a pastry bag fitted with a plain tip or in a plastic squeeze bottle, and refrigerate.

• To serve, cut the limes in half. Slice a bit off the bottom of each lime half so that it will stand upright. Place one lime half in the center of each of 4 plates.

• Arrange 6 of the fig halves around each lime. Loosely drape the ham over the figs. Pipe or squeeze the lime cream over the figs and ham in a thin, lacy pattern. Sprinkle each plate with 1 teaspoon of the chives

"FILET MIGNON" OF RARE TUNA CAPPED WITH SEARED FOIE GRAS ON CHARRED ONIONS AND BURGUNDY BUTTER SAUCE

4 servings

Ingredients for the Burgundy Butter Sauce

1 cup balsamic vinegar

1 1/8 cups red wine

1 shallot, cut in half

1/4 cup cold, unsalted butter, cut into tablespoon-size pieces

Ingredients for the Tuna

1 large white onion, cut into 1/4-inch slices

1/4 cup olive oil

2 quarts lightly salted water

2 large carrots, peeled and sliced very thin lengthwise into ribbons

2 medium zucchini, sliced very thin lengthwise into ribbons

2 tablespoons browned butter (butter cooked to a light hazelnut color)

salt and freshly ground pepper to taste

4 ounces foie gras

4 6-ounce center-cut tuna steaks, trimmed into the shape of filet mignon

Method for the Burgundy Butter Sauce

· Combine the vinegar, wine, and shallot in a medium-size, heavy-bottomed saucepan over medium heat and reduce to a syrupy consistency. Using a wooden spoon, incorporate the butter into the sauce 1 piece at a time. When all the butter is incorporated, remove the shallot pieces. Keep warm until ready to serve.

Method for the Tuna

· Heat a 10-inch cast-iron skillet over high heat until very hot. Moisten the onion slices with some of the olive oil and lay as many of them in the hot skillet as will fit in one layer. Cook until lightly charred, then turn the slices over with tongs and char the other side. Remove the onions from the pan and keep warm. Repeat the process with the remaining onions.

· Meanwhile, bring the salted water to a rapid boil in a large pot and drop in the carrot ribbons. Cook for 2 to 3 minutes, or until the carrots are tender but still firm (al dente). Lift the carrots out of the water with a slotted spoon and place them in a bowl.

· Using the same pot of boiling water, repeat this process with the zucchini ribbons. (The zucchini will cook much faster than the carrots.) Add the zucchini to the bowl with the carrots. Stir in the browned butter and season with salt and pepper.

recipe continued on page 169

- Using a very sharp knife dipped in warm water, cut the foie gras into 1/2-inch-thick slices. Sprinkle the slices with salt and pepper and keep chilled.

- Moisten the tuna steaks with some of the olive oil and season them with salt and pepper. Place them in the same hot skillet used to char the onions and sear on each side for about 2 minutes. Remove the steaks and keep warm.

- In a smoking hot sauté pan, sear the foie gras slices on both sides for about 30 seconds, or just until a crisp outer crust forms. Remove them from the pan and keep warm.

- To serve, quickly lay 3 or 4 charred onion rings in the center of each of 4 warm serving plates. Arrange 2 carrot ribbons and 2 zucchini ribbons over the onions in a nestlike pattern. Place a tuna steak on top, then finish with a slice of foie gras and a few charred onions. Sauce each plate with 3 pools of the burgundy butter sauce.

WARM GRANNY SMITH APPLE TART

6 servings

Ingredients

Basic Pie Dough (recipe on page 171)

2 Granny Smith apples

3 tablespoons unsalted butter

1/2 teaspoon ground cinnamon

2 tablespoons heavy cream

6 tablespoons Southern Comfort

1/3 cup sugar combined with 1 rounded teaspoon ground cinnamon

vanilla ice cream

Method

• Preheat the oven to 400°F.

• On a floured board, roll out the dough to about 1/8 inch thick. Lay a bowl about 5 inches in diameter upside down on the dough. Using the rim as a pattern, cut out 6 circles with a sharp paring knife. Place the pastry rounds between sheets of waxed paper and refrigerate.

• Peel and core the apples, then slice them into 1/8-inch sections. In a large sauté pan, melt the butter over medium heat. Add the apples and cook for several minutes. Add the cinnamon and heavy cream and stir. Carefully add the Southern Comfort, averting your face, since it will ignite. Continue cooking until the apples are soft and pliable.

• Remove the apples with a slotted spoon and place them on a non-reactive baking sheet. Cool in the refrigerator. Simmer the cooking liquid until it is reduced by half. Set this mixture aside to glaze the tarts with after they are baked.

• Remove the pastry rounds from the refrigerator. Spray several baking sheets with nonstick cooking spray and lay the rounds on them. Place the chilled apple slices in concentric circles around each pastry round, leaving a 1/4-inch border at the edges. Roll 1 apple slice into a tight circle to form a rosette, repeat with 5 more apple slices, and place one in the center of each tart. (The tarts may be assembled up to this point and refrigerated.)

• Dust the tarts with cinnamon sugar and bake for about 7 minutes, or until the crust is a rich golden brown. Remove the tarts from the oven and brush with the reserved cooking liquid. Serve the tarts on individual plates with scoops of vanilla ice cream.

BASIC PIE DOUGH

Ingredients

2 cups all-purpose flour

1/3 cup butter

1/3 cup shortening or vegetable oil

1/3 cup ice water

Method

- Sift the flour into a medium-size bowl. Add the butter and shortening or vegetable oil and cut into small pieces with a pastry cutter or 2 knives. Work the mixture with your fingertips until it resembles coarse cornmeal.

- Make a well in the center of the mixture and add the water, kneading until the dough forms a ball. Wrap the dough tightly in plastic wrap and refrigerate for at least 30 minutes. When you are ready to use the dough, roll it out on a lightly floured surface and proceed with your recipe.

TELEVISION SPONSORS

— European-Style Butter —

Anyone who has ever eaten butter in Europe is familiar with its wonderful flavor. It is creamier and more delicious, and has a richer aroma, than butter produced in the United States. The secret is in the slight amount of extra butterfat that it takes to meet European standards. With just 2 percent more butterfat, European butter excels in taste and texture and in its performance in cooking.

Keller's Creamery in Harleysville, Pennsylvania, has been making European-style butter in America for over ten years. The product was developed to accommodate discriminating professional chefs, whose response was so positive that Keller's has recently made its butter available to the public in food stores. Home cooking enthusiasts can now experience the added richness European-style butter will give their recipes. As any chef will attest, there is no substitute for butter in cooking. European-style butter raises the standards even further by improving recipes in a variety of ways. Cakes rise higher, croissants turn out flakier, and sauces are smoother than with traditional butter. European-style butter also has a higher burning point, making it easier to sauté.

Keller's European-Style Butter is available in select food stores. For more information, contact Keller's Creamery, 855 Maple Avenue, Harleysville, PA 19438, or on their Web site at www.butter1.com.

— High-Performance Cutlery and Sharpeners —

Dependable equipment was a key ingredient in the successful filming of *Flavors of America*. Throughout the production, Jim Coleman, his assistants, and guests relied on Chef's Choice products, manufactured by the EdgeCraft Corporation in Avondale, Pennsylvania.

The workmanship and balance of Chef's Choice knives make them comfortable to use, and they are forged with edges that stay sharp up to ten times longer than average cutlery. The key to their performance is the unique composition of Trizor steel. The high carbon and molybdenum content in this steel produces more flexible blades that sharpen to a finer, more durable edge.

Every knife has to be sharpened occasionally, and the Diamond Hone Sharpeners produced by Chef's Choice are widely recognized as top-of-the-line. Their 100 percent diamond abrasive technology and built-in angle guides easily restore sharp edges in seconds. Because Chef's Choice products are designed to last a lifetime, they offer value as well as high quality to professional chefs and discriminating home cooks. For more information about Chef's Choice products, call 1-800-342-3255.

BIBLIOGRAPHY

Adams, Marcia. *New Recipes from Quilt Country: More Food and Folkways from the Amish and Mennonites.* New York: Clarkson Potter, 1997.

Aidells, Bruce, and Denis Kelly. *Real Beer and Good Eats: The Rebirth of America's Beer and Food Traditions.* New York: Alfred A. Knopf, 1992.

Benning, Lee Edwards. *The Cook's Tales: Origins of Famous Foods and Recipes.* Old Saybrook, Conn.: Globe Pequot Press, 1992.

Bissell, Frances. *The Book of Food.* New York: Henry Holt, 1989.

Brown, Dale. *American Cooking.* Alexandria, Va.: Time-Life Books, 1968.

Chalmers, Irena. *The Great Food Almanac: A Feast of Facts from A to Z.* San Francisco: Collins, 1994.

Claiborne, Craig. *The New York Times Food Encyclopedia.* New York: Times Books, 1985.

Cox, Beverly, and Martin Jacobs. *Spirit of the Harvest: North American Indian Cooking.* New York: Stewart, Tabori & Chang, 1991.

Czarnecki, Jack. *A Cook's Book of Mushrooms.* New York: Artisan, 1995.

Fortin, Jacques. *The Visual Food Encyclopedia: The Definitive Practical Guide to Food and Cooking.* New York: Macmillan, 1996.

Grossinger, Jennie. *The Art of Jewish Cooking.* New York: Bantam Books, 1960.

Grossman, Harold J. *Grossman's Guide to Wines, Spirits, and Beers.* New York: Charles Scribner's Sons, 1964.

Grunwald, Henry Anatole. *Vegetables.* The Good Cook Techniques and Recipes Series. Alexandria, Va.: Time-Life Books, 1979.

Herbst, Sharon Tyler. *The New Food Lover's Companion.* Hauppauge, N.Y.: Barron's Educational Series, 1995.

Hom, Ken. *Fragrant Harbor Taste: The New Chinese Cooking of Hong Kong.* New York: Simon and Schuster, 1989.

Hom, Ken. *The Taste of China.* London: Bracken Books, 1994.

Hurley, Judith Benn. *The Good Herb: Recipes and Remedies from Nature.* New York: William Morrow, 1995.

Jenkins, Steven. *Cheese Primer.* New York: Workman, 1996.

Jones, Evan. *American Food: The Gastronomic Story.* Woodstock, N.Y.: Overlook Press, 1990.

Krondl, Michael. *Around the American Table: Treasured Recipes and Food Traditions from the American Cookery Collections of the New York Public Library.* Holbrook, Mass.: Adams Media Corporation, 1995.

Mariani, John F. *The Dictionary of American Food and Drink.* New York: Hearst Books, 1994.

Marquis, Vivienne, and Patricia Haskell. *The Cheese Book: The Definitive Guide to the Cheeses of the World.* New York: Simon and Schuster, Fireside, 1964.

McClaine, A. J. *The Encyclopedia of Fish Cookery.* New York: Holt, Rinehart & Winston, 1977.

Morton, Mark. *Cupboard Love: A Dictionary of Culinary Curiosities.* Winnipeg, Canada: Bain & Cox, 1996.

Nanovic, John. *The Complete Book of Wines, Vineyards & Labels.* United States of America: Ottenheimer, 1979.

Roberson, John and Marie. *The Complete Barbecue Book.* New York: Prentice-Hall, 1951.

Root, Waverly. *Food: An Authoritative and Visual History and Dictionary of the Foods of the World.* New York: Konecky & Konecky, 1980.

Shields, John. *The Chesapeake Bay Cookbook: Rediscovering the Pleasures of Great Regional Cuisine.* Reading, Mass.: Addison Wesley, 1990.

Simon, Andre L., and Robin Howe. *Dictionary of Gastronomy.* New York: McGraw-Hill, 1970.

Tannahill, Reay. *Food in History.* New York: Crown, 1988.

Toussaint-Samat, Maguelonne. *History of Food.* Cambridge, Mass.: Blackwell, 1994.

Weaver, William Woys. *Pennsylvania Dutch Country Cooking.* New York: Abbeville Press, 1993.

Wolfe, Linda. *The Cooking of the Caribbean Islands.* New York: Time-Life Books, 1970.

INDEX